THE Dim Sum BOOK

中國點心書

Classic Recipes from the Chinese Teahouse

DRAWINGS BY LAUREN JARRETT

CALLIGRAPHY BY SAN YAN WONG

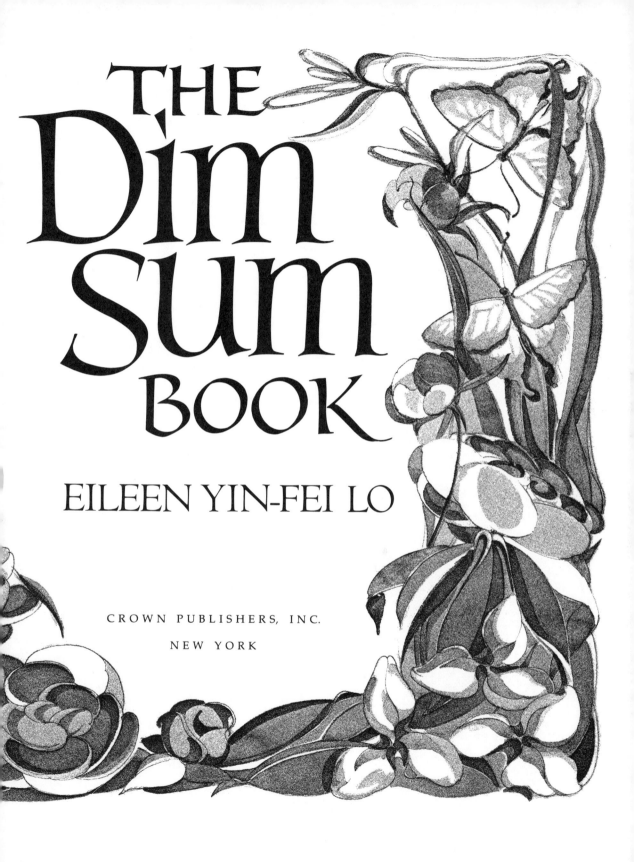

THE Dim Sum BOOK

EILEEN YIN-FEI LO

CROWN PUBLISHERS, INC.

NEW YORK

Published by Crown Publishers, Inc.,
One Park Avenue, New York, New York 10016,
and simultaneously in Canada
by General Publishing Company Limited
Manufactured in the United States of America
Library of Congress Cataloging in Publication Data
Lo, Eileen Yin-Fei.
The dim sum book.
Includes index.
1. Cookery, Chinese.   2. Snack foods.   I. Title.
TX724.5.C5L5945 1982   641.5951   81-19608
ISBN: 0-517-54581-0   AACR2
Book design by Camilla Filancia
10 9 8 7 6 5 4 3 2 1
First Edition

This book could not have been completed were it not for the patience and stomach capacities of my family, which sat through interminable tasting and testing sessions. We ate and argued and laughed, occasionally we fought, always we loved.

Thank you, Stephen, Elena, Christopher, and Fred.

Contents

Acknowledgments

The family, after all, couldn't eat them *all* and so, as I experimented, before deciding eventually which dim sum pleased me most, the efforts of those experiments went forth. I thank my students, my neighbors and friends, my local fire department, Lauren Jarrett, and finally, my editor, Pamela Thomas, for their willing appetites.

A thank you is in order as well to those dim sum chefs who gave me so much encouragement and bits of their knowledge, but my very special gratitude goes to San Yan Wong, my occasional teacher and private calligrapher.

Finally I thank my agent Joseph Spieler, who told me early on, "You cook, I'll sell," and he did.

YUM CHA
The Dim Sum Teahouse

飲
茶

Fred's Special Pancake

Glutinous Rice

Congee

Glutinous Rice Loaf

Spare Ribs

Stuffed Lotus Leaves

Introduction

The earliest memory I have of dim sum is of the time when I was four years old and lived in Siu Lo Cheun, or "Lo's Little Village," a town bearing my family's name in the suburban Cantonese region of Sun Tak.

My eighteen-year-old brother, Ching Mo, had won a rather large sum of money after many hours of mah-jongg and he came bursting happily into our house, grabbed me by the hands, lifted me onto his shoulders, and shouted, "Let's go to yum cha!"

Now, *yum cha* means literally to "drink tea," but I knew he wasn't just going to treat me to a cup of Bo Lei Cha, prized though it was. Yum cha meant to drink tea but it also meant to "eat dim sum," the different and delicious small teahouse foods that we loved so much. To eat dim sum in our family was quite a treat. Dim sum was customarily not made in the home; it was teahouse food, and it was doubly a treat because the only teahouse in Siu Lo Cheun, like most other Cantonese teahouses, was only for men.

The teahouse was where men came to talk with other men, about sugarcane crops and farming, about the fish they had caught and those they missed. They read their newspapers and conducted business, and those who were retired or wealthy enough not to have to work would bring their pet birds and spend mornings in the teahouse at leisure.

It wasn't exactly that women were forbidden to go into teahouses, it was just that they *didn't*, by tradition. Even somewhat liberated women like my mother, Miu How, one of the very few women of Sun Tak to

4

Stuffed Mushrooms	Stuffed Bean Curd	Stuffed Peppers
Spring Roll	Fresh Rice Noodle	Cured Ham in Cabbage
Sausage Bun	Egg Custard Tart	Pearl Balls
Taro Root Horn	Shrimp Toast	Phoenix Eyes
Baked Pork Bun	Turnip Cake	Shrimp Dumpling

Steamed Pork Bun

Red Bean Pastry
Turnip Pastry

Curried Chicken Pastry

Scallion Pancake

Stuffed Crab Claw

Shrimp Balls

Good Luck Dumpling
Rice Noodle Fruit

Water Dumpling

Siu Mai

Orchid Sculpture

Butterfly Sculpture

Dove Sculpture

Four-Seasons Sculpture

Frog Sculpture

Goldfish Sculpture

refuse the traditional foot bindings of upper-class females, would not go into a teahouse. Once a girl became ten years old or so, the teahouse became out of bounds. Goggled-eyed little girls of four, simultaneously happy and apprehensive, like me, however, were allowed in simply because they were little.

I remember the teahouse in Siu Lo Cheun as being one big room with many windows and many tables scattered around, all of them occupied by men. Memories of the room are vague, but memories of what I ate are vivid, vivid because I always ate the same things when my brother took me there: *char siu bau*, soft, fluffy steamed dough buns filled with small pieces of roast pork; *har gau*, half-moon-shaped dumplings filled with chopped shrimp; *siu mai*, basket-shaped dumplings of minced shrimp, pork, and mushrooms, and *pai gwat siu mai*, tiny morsels of spare ribs in a black bean sauce. To this day they are my favorite dim sum.

When I was twelve and left Siu Lo Cheun for Hong Kong, I went into a different world. Teahouses were social centers and many of them were vast, barnlike, multistoried restaurants that were places for families, including women. They were where you went during the New Year holiday, for the Dragon Boat Festival days of May, for the August Moon, sometimes for birthdays and almost always on Sundays.

My mother and father sent me away from our town during the New Year's school vacation in 1950 because of the revolution in China. They would not leave their home and lands but they wanted their daughter safe in Hong Kong. They were correct. I was spared the violence but not the sorrow, however, because my brother, who had taken me to the teahouse when I was four, died in Siu Lo Cheun's corner of that revolution two years after I left.

I lived in Kowloon for a while with a distant aunt, my father's number-five sister, and I remember going to the Nathan Tea House, one of those big places, more than once. I don't quite remember what it looked like, but my feeling is that I didn't *care* what it looked like, because it was where I could get those char siu bau that I loved. And I did. Subsequently I lived with what I call a consortium of cousins out in the New Territories area of Fanling, about twenty miles from Kowloon. Our teahouse there was modest but occasionally I got to go out to Tai Po as a chaperon to one of my cousins and her young man friend. The teahouse there was bigger, with more dim sum, and though I didn't particularly care about being a chaperon, the food, I remember, was very, very good.

It was back to Kowloon, where I stayed with my father's number-six sister, my aunt Look Gu Jeh, with whom I lived until I came to the United States. Look Gu Jeh, a splendid cook filled with the tradition of fine cooking that permeates Sun Tak (where it is said the finest cooks in China come from), taught me much.

I had begun cooking at the age of six, learning a bit from my mother, but mostly from my father, Pak Wan, who was a marvelous and meticulous chef. I was taught steaming and stir-frying while quite young, and the combination of elements that make for flavor. It was my father who insisted that I take each individual bean sprout, for example, and break off its ends so that the spring rolls he was teaching me to create would contain only the crunchy white centers of the sprout. Oh, how I hated doing that! It seemed to be a chore that took hours.

Because going to our teahouse was a rare thing, we cooked a good many of what are classical dim sum preparations at home. At the age of seven I made *dai gut yau gor*, "Good Luck Dumplings," before Chinese New Year, and a year later I made my first turnip cake, which I remember eating with pickled red ginger. I also learned to make glutinous rice dumplings covered with sesame seeds and it was I who went to the town bakery to buy the fresh bread with which to make shrimp toasts. I learned many dim sum preparations from Look Gu Jeh and I continued to make many of them in the United States. In fact I teach dim sum cookery now, and with each class it becomes a more enjoyable science as my students discover that they can be apprentice artists of the teahouse. And they go into the many dim sum teahouses now existing in America, their families trailing after them, confident in their ability to judge and to enjoy a food that once was total mystery.

In the teahouses of Hong Kong, even today, and in the dim sum restaurants that have sprung up in other countries, it is not an uncommon sight to see four generations of a Chinese family around a yum cha table, drinking tea, eating uncountable varieties of dim sum, and chattering. True, there are still quite traditional teahouses, certainly in Canton and Hong Kong, places like Hing Wan in Hong Kong that still provide racks from which the wealthy at leisure can hang their birdcages while they enjoy dim sum, but the dim sum restaurant is for groups of shopgirls as well to enjoy their lunch. Dim sum is for everybody.

Perhaps because of the misty rosiness that surrounds the history of tea, dim sum, the food that accompanies tea, has emerged as the most romantic aspect of that most sophisticated Cantonese cookery. Even its name is soft and lovely. Dim sum, literally translated, means "a point on the heart" or "a dot on the heart," and its gastronomic interpretation has come to be "a delight of the heart" or "a touch of the heart's delight." Lu Yu would like any of them.

A Few Words About Tea

Lu Yu is China's historical Master of Tea who in the eighth century wrote his *Classic of Tea*, which set down for the first time how tea leaves should be grown and processed, how tea should be brewed and steeped, how it should be served, how to create a tea caddy. Tea, Lu Yu wrote, was drink for both the body and soul, a mental stimulant, perhaps the way to immortality. And from his work all manner of tea observances proceeded.

Of course tea had been part of Chinese historical myth before Lu Yu's time. For example, some believe that tea was the serendipitous discovery of the Emperor Shen Nung during the third century B.C. How? Well, it seemed the Emperor liked his drinking water boiled and one day as it was aboil a camellia blossom fell into it. The aroma was captivating and forced him to taste the first pot of tea ever made. To this day the Chinese add camellias, rose and orange blossoms, the flowers of the lychee and the orange tree, and various other petals to tea.

Generally, it is believed that tea was first cultivated in China but with bushes brought back from India by a Han Dynasty scholar in the second century A.D., but evidence exists that tea as a soul-satisfying substance was very much a part of Chinese life before that time. Those who dispute the India theory suggest that tea, as a cultivated bush, originated in Hunan, later in Szechuan, as a member of the camellia family. What has emerged as the lore of Chinese tea, however, began with Lu Yu, who decreed that tea should be in cakes, that a bit of salt should be added to the boiling water used to brew the tea, and that the brewed tea should be served only in bowls of underglaze blue. Tea later was ground into powder; still later, dried leaves, after roasting to seal in the flavor, were used as the basis for pots of tea. And tea became a drink for all the people, not just for the privileged.

Most tea drunk in China and Hong Kong, and elsewhere, these days is brewed from those little curled and dried leaves, although powdered teas and those in brick form are used occasionally. And though the Chinese have never developed an elaborate, ritualistic tea ceremony as have the Japanese, they *do* follow the dictates of Lu Yu, rules that in practical terms result in the best tea making.

What he said to do was place an earthenware vessel on a smokeless fire of charcoal, not just any charcoal as you might suppose, but charcoal made from olive pits. Water from a slow-moving stream should be put into the pot and boiled. Rushing water was bad for the throat, he said, and still water was not even to be considered. Once boiled, the water should be poured into a porcelain cup over the tea leaves, then most of it poured out, then fresh water should be added. Only then is the tea drinkable. He then suggested that it be drunk in the company of beautiful women in a pavilion next to a water lily pond or near a lacquered bridge.

Few of us have pavilions or water lily ponds or lacquered bridges, but we can brew tea well enough to enjoy it thoroughly. Water for tea should be drawn fresh from the tap (slowly moving) and then boiled until the first bubbles appear. The teapot (earthenware) should be preheated with boiling water, then the leaves, 1 teaspoon of loose tea per person and 1 for the pot, should be placed in it. Pour the boiling water in and allow it to steep from 3 to 6 minutes, the longer the stronger; then serve in porcelain cups.

From the hundreds of teas that are available in Chinese food shops, from shops such as Fortnum & Mason in England, which was founded on a base of Chinese tea imports, from Chinese herbalists, have come the teas that are most familiar to the teahouse. They are:

Lung Ching is a green tea, often called Dragon Well, that is grown on the hillsides around Hangzhou, and it is regarded as the crowning achievement of Chinese tea-growing. It is used regularly in China at state dinners, costs about twelve dollars an ounce, and must be drunk when it is only a few months old. It does not keep, and after a year it loses every bit of its character, which is fresh, light, and green. The Chinese say that Lung Ching stimulates the appetite and is also a perfect remedy for the body when it is suffering from an excess of "hot elements," dry mouth and throat, dry nostrils and red eyes, which accurately describes running a fever. I also use Dragon Well tea to make tea-smoked duck. It imparts an absolutely breathtaking smokiness to the meat.

Shou Mae is a strong, unfermented tea. The leaves are hand-picked, massaged between the palms, and wind-dried, never in the sun. Once brewed the tea has a bitter taste. The Chinese regard it as quite good for respiration and for the relief of bronchial complications.

Bo Lei, the tea of my childhood and the favorite of the Cantonese, seems to get better as it gets older. In Hong Kong it is possible to buy hundred-year-old cakes of Bo Lei. The Cantonese love Bo Lei with dim sum because it is perfect, they believe, for digestion and as an ulcer preventative. It has a hearty and robust taste.

Jasmine is a clean-tasting tea that cleanses the palate and goes quite well with highly flavored or spicy foods. The Chinese say it is just fine as a cure for a stomach ache.

Chrysanthemum is also a tea that is believed to keep the palate clear. It is available in flower form and as a crystal and is supposed to be very good for the liver, the nerves, and the eyes.

Soi Sin is one of the many oolong teas favored in China. This comes from Fukien Province, is greenish-brown in color, and tastes slightly bitter. Some Chinese use it as a morning wake-up drink as well as with dim sum.

Tiht Koon Yum, which is the Cantonese pronunciation of Teh Kuan Yin, is the name of China's mythological Iron Goddess of Mercy. This is another of the oolongs and it derives its name from its dark, metallic green color. Actually it is very similar to Soi Sin and is regarded as a stimulant.

Look On is a black tea that looks quite strong but actually is very mild after it is brewed. It is called Cloud Mist and is highly regarded by the elderly, whose digestion, it is said, cannot abide the stronger teas.

Green teas such as *Dragon Well* and *Shou Mae* are not fermented, they are dried; while black teas like *Bo Lei* and *Look On* are made from fermented leaves which oxidize and turn black during the drying process. The oolongs are a combination of the two processes, the fermentation process being interrupted so that the leaves become dark black-green. The flower teas are generally green teas to which the flowers and petals are added.

Tea, Lu Yu suggested, is a wonder, "if one is feeling hot, given to melancholia, suffering from aching of the brain, smarting of the eyes, trouble in the forelimbs or afflicted in one hundred joints, he may take tea four or five times a day, the liquor is like the sweetest dew of heaven." And it goes beautifully with food.

Imagine yourself in the Luk Yu Teahouse on Stanley Street in Hong Kong, a teahouse bearing the Cantonese version of Lu Yu's name. It is surely the most splendid of the traditional Chinese teahouses, more than a half-century old, with carved blackwood furniture, marble-topped tables, slowly circulating ceiling fans, screens, booths enclosed by carved wood walls and exquisitely etched glass. You have come in, gone up to the second floor because it is quieter than the street level, seated yourself, and asked for a pot of jasmine tea. It is brought, along with teacups and a bowl a bit larger than a rice bowl. You pour some tea into the bowl and then roll each of the teacups through it, using the boiled tea to cleanse your teacups. The bowl is removed and you pour your jasmine into the teacups and you sip and wait.

Soon you hear the singsong.

"Har Gau, Siu Mai, H-a-r G-au, Si-u Ma-i," the women's voices call out softly as the *dim sum mui,* the "dim sum maids," wheel carts among the tables, calling out what is in the steamers and pots. "Pai Gwat Siu Mai, Woo Gok, Pa-i Gwat Si-u Ma-i, W-oo-oo G-ok." The maid does not ask if you want what she has, she sings. It is up to you to call out, to point at what you like, and she will serve the dim sum in tiny dishes or bamboo steamers.

It goes on.

"Char Siu Bau, Lor Bok Oh, Gai See Geun, Char Si-u B-au, Lor B-o-k Ohhh, G-ai S-ee Ge-un."

You eat, you sample. The dishes pile up. Your teapot is empty. So you flip the lid backward so it rests on the handle and your waiter knows to bring a fresh pot of tea. Perhaps as he pours you are talking. There is no need to thank him, just tap four fingers of your hand on the tabletop and he will acknowledge that you have thanked him with the unobtrusive etiquette of the teahouse.

And the food!

Half-moons of pastry, tiny steamed dough baskets, translucent squares of cakes made with water chestnuts, triangles of fresh bean curd, pancakes laced with scallions, tiny pillows filled with shrimp, mounds of rice wrapped in the leaves of lotus and bamboo, dumplings like corkscrews, horns, rolls, cylinders, balls of meat dotted with pearls of rice, cakes, tarts, the shapes and textures and tastes seem endless as they pass in wondrous parade.

The beginnings of the informal and variegated dim sum meal go back to the Sung Dynasty, according to some historians, when tenth-century travelers along the highways of China began stopping at small roadside teahouses to refresh themselves en route to their destinations with light meals and tea. But centuries were required before the practice could take root, because two hundred years earlier, during Lu Yu's time, tea was really not an accompaniment to food, or vice versa. It was pure, a serene drink, a contemplative liquid, usually drunk quietly in private.

But the very practical discoveries of the benefits of tea upon diet, its aid as a digestive, its ability to cleanse the palate, its very real grease- and oil-cutting properties, soon made a marriage. Tea and food came together and the brief meal in the teahouse came soon after. And the foods evolved, as do most things in China, out of a combined mythological and historical perspective. A poet once threw himself into a river in protest and his supporters tossed rice and meat wrapped in bamboo leaves after him. These were called *jongtzu* and a Cantonese version, *nor mai gai,* is served to this day in teahouses. Then there is *dai gut yau gor,* which literally are "New Year's horns," also called "Good Luck Dumplings," and are made of brown sugar, pulverized peanuts, and sesame seeds. And there was the petty official named Kuai who ordered the death of a popular soldier. In protest people put together two sticks of dough and put them in oil, calling them *yau ja kwai,* "oil-fried Kuais." Today they are found in teahouses and are considered Chinese crullers.

Southern China in general and Canton in particular became the natural home for dim sum and the practice of yum cha. It is a phenomenon but barely known in the northern centers of the country. Dim sum is Cantonese, with touches of Shanghai here and there, and Hong Kong, because it is basically Cantonese, is the quintessential dim sum city.

Its teahouses are large, good-natured restaurants that are hospitable, noisy, often boisterous with celebrations of all sorts, and redolent with the continually changing aromas of freshly made dim sum. Families and friends, and business acquaintances, sit around vast circular tables, talking and eating, arguing, baiting and teasing, ordering from the maid when the mood strikes them. The Cantonese like to talk, often all of them together it seems, and in the dim sum teahouses that's what they do. But they also eat—bountifully—and they drink tea, much tea, all of it to delight the heart.

點心廚房 The Dim Sum Kitchen

The Foods

基本食品

Dim sum is a specialized Chinese cuisine and as such requires some ingredients not readily available at your local supermarket. Most of the foodstuffs of Chinese origin are, however, easily obtainable at Chinese and other Asian groceries and I have noticed with some gratification that more and more specialty food shops as well as larger general-purpose markets are stocking the foods used in Chinese cookery.

For dim sum, with its heavy accent on the fashioning of dough, you will need the customary ingredients needed in baking, such as baking powder, baking soda, evaporated milk, lard and vegetable shortenings, dried yeast, and of course, flour. There seems no need to list all of them because they are common to most kitchens.

I have avoided listing products by brand name except in instances where I feel the quality of a particular brand is quite superior. The primary exception is with flours. The flours I prefer are quite specific by brand, the result of much testing and baking under all seasonal and temperature conditions.

Here then are the foods you will need to make dim sum:

竹筍 **Bamboo Shoots.**
Though these come canned in various ways, I prefer bamboo shoots cut into large chunks, so that I can cut them to my own specifications. They are crisp and yellowish and once removed from the can can be kept

15

in glass jars or plastic containers. Refrigerated and kept in water that is changed daily, they will keep 4 to 6 weeks.

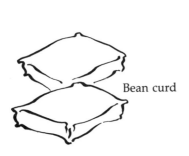

Bean curd

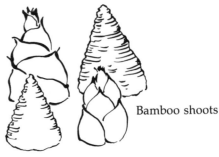

Bamboo shoots

Bean Curd.
These come in square cakes, 2½ to 3 inches to a square. Made from soybeans, they are white and have a consistency like custard. I prefer the fresh, individual cakes rather than those that come several to a package, as they are sometimes sold. Bean curd has little taste of its own and its versatility lies in its ability to absorb the tastes of other substances. Kept refrigerated in a container, the water of which should be changed daily, it will keep 2 to 3 weeks.

Bean sprouts

Bean Sprouts.
These are white, plump, and crunchy and are grown from mung beans. They are sold by weight in Chinese groceries, and they can be stored in plastic bags into which holes have been punched. Storage must be in the refrigerator and they can be kept usually no more than 4 days, after which they lose their color and their firmness.

Black Beans, Fermented.
These beans, usually preserved in salt, are wonderfully fragrant and tasty. Though they come in plastic packages and cans, I prefer those in packages slightly seasoned with orange peel and ginger. Before using,

salt should be rinsed off. They can be kept for as long as a year, without refrigeration, as long as they are in a tightly sealed container.

白
菜

Bok Choy.

This word is Cantonese for "white vegetable" and describes best the white-stalked, green-leafed vegetable that is so versatile and so useful in Chinese cookery. It is sold by weight, and the taste is sweet and juicy. Although it is occasionally called "Chinese cabbage," I think that is a misnomer because it truly is not like a cabbage at all. It will keep for about a week in the vegetable drawer of the refrigerator, but it tends to lose its sweetness quickly, so I recommend using it when it is fresh.

天
津
白
菜

Celery Cabbage.

Often called Tientsin bok choy, this comes in two varieties, either with a long stalk or a rounder sort which is much leafier. The latter is most often referred to as Tientsin bok choy, and I prefer it because it is the sweeter of the two. It is also at its best in the spring. It may be kept, refrigerated, in a plastic bag for about a week, but like bok choy, it tends to lose its sweetness, so I suggest using it early, if not at once.

Bok choy or Chinese lettuce

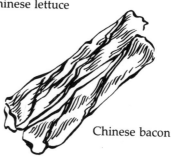

Chinese bacon

Chinese Bacon.

This bacon is marinated, while raw, in molasses and thick soy sauce and salt and then sun-dried. It is sold by weight in thick slices and must be cooked before eating. In China, because it is pork, and raw, it is used only in winter when it is cold. It can be stored, refrigerated, for a week but can be frozen for from 3 to 4 months.

Chinese Black Mushrooms.

These dried mushrooms come in boxes or in cellophane packs. They are black, dark gray, or speckled in color and range in size from those with caps about the size of a nickel to those with diameters of 3 inches. Those in boxes are choicest, both in size and color, and, of course, they are more expensive. Chinese black mushrooms must always be soaked in hot water for at least 1/2 hour before use, their stems removed and discarded, and they should be thoroughly cleaned on the underside of the cap and squeezed dry. In their dried form they will keep indefinitely in a tightly closed container. If you live in an especially damp or humid climate they should be stored in the freezer.

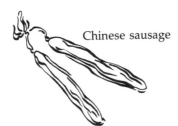

Chinese sausage

Chinese black mushrooms

Chinese Sausages.

These are traditionally made in China of pork, pork liver, and duck liver. Very little duck liver sausage is available in the United States, however. Most common is pork sausages, usually in pairs, threaded through with pork fat, and held together by string. They are cured, but not cooked, and thus must be cooked before eating. They can be kept refrigerated for about a month and frozen from 3 to 4 months. A somewhat leaner pork sausage from Canadian processors is also available in some markets, but in my view it lacks the distinctive flavor of those made in the United States.

Chinese White Turnips.

Large and white, 8 inches or longer, 2 to 3 inches thick, these have

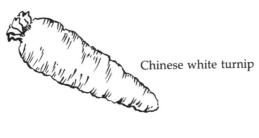

Chinese white turnip

a lovely crispness and the nearly hot tang of radishes. They will keep for a week in the refrigerator vegetable drawer, but are best used early.

Coriander.

Also called cilantro, and "Chinese parsley," this is almost identical in appearance to flat-leaf or Italian parsley. It has a strong aroma and taste, and, used either as a seasoning agent or as a garnish, it is distinctive. Often it is suggested that Italian parsley be used as a substitute. To me there is no substitute for this herb. It should be used quickly so that its bouquet will be appreciated, but it can be kept refrigerated for a week to 10 days.

Curry Powder.

There are many brands of curry powder on the market. I prefer the stronger, more pungent brands from India, but I believe that among domestically packaged curries, Crosse & Blackwell is preferable, particularly because of its heavy reliance on coriander.

Five-Spice Powder.

A powder that imparts a distinctive taste of anise to food. It can be made of a combination of spices including star anise, fennel seeds, cinnamon, cloves, ginger root, licorice, nutmeg, and Szechuan peppercorns. Obviously there are more than 5 spices listed, but different makers use different combinations. However, anise and cinnamon predominate in all the blends.

Flour.

There are many brands of flour available but I have chosen four, after much testing, as ideal for dim sum doughs. They will be discussed in greater detail subsequently. They are:

Pillsbury's Best Bread Flour, enriched, bromated, naturally white, high protein, high gluten
Pillsbury's Best, all-purpose, enriched, bleached
Pillsbury's H & R (sold in 25-pound bags to hotels and restaurants, but which Pillsbury says is identical to its All-Purpose)
Gold Medal All-Purpose, enriched, bleached, presifted

Food Colorings.

Yellow, orange, red, and green coloring will be needed, but be certain to buy natural colorings only.

Ginger Root.

A substance you cannot do without in Chinese cookery. When selecting ginger roots, look for those with smooth outer skins, because like many of us, ginger begins to wrinkle and roughen with age. It seasons, it is used to diffuse strong fish and shellfish odors, and the Chinese say that it greatly reduces stomach acidity. It is used rather sparingly and should be peeled and sliced before use. Placed in a heavy brown paper bag and refrigerated, it will keep for from 4 to 6 weeks. I do not recommend trying to preserve it in wine or freezing it, because either way it loses strength. Nor do I recommend powdered ginger or bottled ginger juice as cooking substitutes, because for ginger there is no substitute.

Ginger root

Glutinous Rice.

Often called "Sweet Rice," this is shorter grained than usual rice and when cooked becomes somewhat sticky. Its kernels stick together in a mass instead of separating the way long-grain rice does.

Glutinous Rice Powder.

This flour, ground from glutinous rice, provides great elasticity when used as a dough base.

Hoisin Sauce.

This thick, chocolate-brown sauce is made from soy beans, garlic, sugar, and chilies. Some brands add a touch of vinegar, others are thickened with flour. It is best known as a complement to Peking Duck. It comes either in cans or jars and will keep indefinitely when refrigerated in glass jars.

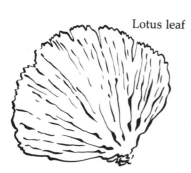

Lotus leaf

Bamboo leaves

Lotus Leaves or Bamboo Leaves.

These dried leaves are used as wrappings for various steamed preparations. Lotus leaves impart a distinctive, somewhat sweet taste and aroma to the food they are wrapped around and are preferred to bamboo leaves. However, lotus leaves are usually sold commercially only to restaurants in 50-pound boxes. Bamboo leaves can be easily bought in smaller quantities and are admirable substitutes, although they have a very different taste and smell. Kept in a plastic bag in a dry place the dried leaves will keep 6 months to a year.

NOTE: If you can get fresh lotus leaves then by all means use them fresh, or sun-dry them yourself for future use.

Lotus Seeds.

The olive-shaped seeds that come from the lotus pod are regarded as a delicacy and priced accordingly, by weight. They can be kept for as long as a month in a tightly sealed jar at room temperature, but I don't recommend it because their texture roughens and their flavor weakens.

Oyster Sauce.

A somewhat thick sauce, the base of which is ground dried oysters, this is used generously by the Cantonese to add color to preparations and to accent flavors. It can be kept indefinitely, if refrigerated in a tightly sealed container. At room temperature, if it is used repeatedly, it will keep for at least a year.

皮
蛋

Preserved Eggs.
Often called *pei dan,* or thousand-year eggs, these are raw eggs, packed in alkali and mud for from 60 to 100 days. The coating penetrates the shell and turns the white and the yolk deep green and brownish-black. The egg is eaten, or used, raw, but the coating must be removed carefully and the egg washed thoroughly before use. Sealed in airtight plastic bags they will keep for 1 to 2 months in the refrigerator.

Preserved eggs

紅　紅
荳　荳
沙

Red Beans.
These small deep-red beans are used generally in sweet preparations although occasionally they are combined with meats in casserole dishes. However, red beans are usually used in paste form, as fillings. The paste comes in cans or it can be made from the dried beans. The beans are sold in plastic sacks by weight and will keep indefinitely.

沾
米

Rice.
For the southern part of China, rice is a life-sustaining staple. In dim sum preparations three kinds of rice are used:

Long-grain Rice is the most widely used rice. It grows in profusion around Canton and in the southern part of China. The best long-grains in the United States come from Texas and Louisiana.

Short-grain Rice is generally cheaper and of a lesser quality than long-grain rice. It is used to make rice-based congees, and the dried form is ground up for rice powder.

Glutinous Rice is a type of short-grain rice and is much richer and heavier than other rices. It is sometimes referred to as "sweet rice" because of its sugary flavor. It, too, can be ground and made into glutinous rice powder.

沙
河
粉

Rice Noodle.
Known as "sah hor fun," to the Cantonese, or "Sand River noodle,"

this is not strictly a noodle. It does not come in strands or bunches, but rather in sheets, both square and round. It is snowy white with a glistening, shiny surface when bought fresh—as it should be—and is usually oiled and folded before packing. Before using, the noodle must be carefully unfolded and whichever size pieces you need cut from it. It cannot be stored at room temperature, but must be refrigerated (and will keep 3 days) or frozen (it will keep 1 to 2 months). After refrigeration or freezing, it must be brought to room temperature and steamed to restore its pliability. Rice noodle is sold in noodle factories in Chinese areas of cities, but some food shops will purchase it for you on request.

Rice Powder.

Flour made from grinding short-grain rice, usually, which is the practice in Canton, though long-grained rice is also ground to powder in the United States. It is usually used in cakes or in doughs used for some dim sum wrappers.

Sesame Oil.

An aromatic oil with a strong, almost nutlike smell that is used both as a cooking oil and as an additive and dressing. Adding a bit of it to an already prepared dish imparts fine flavor, particularly in the case of some congees. It is thick and brown when it comes from China or Japan, thinner and lighter from the Middle East. I recommend using one of the former. It may be stored at room temperature in a tightly capped bottle.

Sesame Seeds.

Black and white. Black seeds, either roasted or not, are customarily used as decorations or in the preparations of sweet fillings. White seeds, roasted, are generally used in dumpling fillings or as garnishes. They are also used in raw form as an ingredient and occasionally in the making of sweets as well.

Shrimp, Dried.

These are small shrimp, dried and salted for preservation. Before using they should be soaked in warm water for at least a half hour. They will keep for 2 or 3 months in a tightly closed container kept in a dry place. They can also be frozen for storage if they are not used often. They should be orange-pink in color, and a sure sign that they are aging and losing their strength is their change to a grayish color.

Soy Sauces.

Light or dark. The light soys are usually taken from the top of the batches being prepared, the darker soys from the bottom. Both are made of soy beans, flour, salt, and water. There are many brands, but my favorite is Yuet Heung Yuen, made in Hong Kong. The light soy from this maker is labeled "Pure Soy Bean Sauce," the dark soy (actually double-dark as it is often called) is marked either " 'A' Soy Sauce" or " 'C' Soy Sauce." Dark soys are best with meats, for roasting, for sauces, for rich and dark coloring. Light soys are best for shrimp, chicken, and pork, and the Chinese believe they give a sweetness of taste to these foods. I often combine the two soys for different tastes and colorings.

Tapioca Flour.

Often called tapioca starch, this is made from the starch of the cassava root, and much of it comes packaged from Thailand. It is used both as a basis for particular dim sum doughs and as a thickener for sauces, as a substitute for cornstarch.

Taro Root.

This starchy root of the tropical taro plant, which is called poi in Hawaii, is somewhat like a potato but is more fibrous and is tinged throughout with purple threads. It must be eaten cooked, usually steamed, and as it steams it emits a chestnutlike aroma.

Taro root

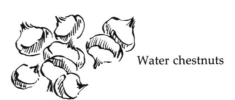
Water chestnuts

Water Chestnuts.

These grow in mud and water, but when washed off, peeled, and cleaned they are the crunchiest of nuts. They are available fresh, which are most desirable, or canned. Fresh and unpeeled they will keep, refrigerated and in a brown paper bag, for 4 to 6 weeks. Canned water chestnuts will keep, refrigerated, in water changed daily, in a tight container for 2 to 3 weeks.

馬
蹄
粉

Water Chestnut Powder.
Used to make cakes and as a thickener for sauces. Sauces with this powder added will give foods over which they are poured a shiny, glazed appearance.

澄
麵
粉

Wheat Starch.
The remains of wheat flour when the wheat's protein is removed to make gluten, this starch is the basis for several dim sum wrappings. Vegetable starches and powders will keep for at least a year if placed in a tightly sealed container and kept in a dry place.

飡俱 The Tools

If one considers the number and variety of recipes that exist in dim sum cookery it is consequently surprising, and gratifying, to learn that only a few utensils are required to prepare them. Following are those that you will need and you will undoubtedly find that most of them are already in your kitchen.

Wok.

This is the all-purpose Chinese cooking utensil that can be used for stir-frying, deep-frying, and blanching. With the addition of a bamboo steamer it is foolproof for dim sum steaming. I recommend carbon-steel woks; a wok 14 inches in diameter is the most convenient size. The seasoning and care of your wok will be discussed in the section on cooking techniques.

A wok, wok lid, and wok ring

Wok Ring.

A steel, hollow base that fits over a single stove burner. The wok sits within it, thus allowing the flame or heat source to envelope the bottom of the wok.

Steamer.

These come in various sizes, but I prefer one 12 to 13 inches in diameter. They can be stacked two or three high and topped with a cover of tightly woven bamboo.

Steamers are usually bamboo, but they are also made of aluminum. In addition, you can buy small, individual steamers of bamboo or stainless steel.

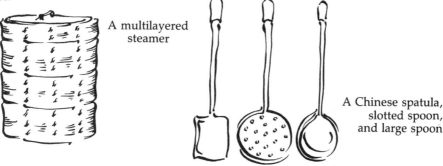

A multilayered steamer

A Chinese spatula, slotted spoon, and large spoon

Chinese Spatula.

A shovel-shaped tool that is available either in carbon or stainless steel and in different sizes. I prefer a medium-size carbon-steel spatula.

Chinese Cleaver.

This is another all-purpose tool. It cuts and dices, and its blade and its handle can mash. Usually made of carbon steel, it is also available in stainless. The carbon steel is preferred because of its keener edge and because it is capable of such heavy-duty jobs as cleaving through bone. The preferred size is one with a blade 8 inches long and between 3½ and 3¾ inches wide.

You may wish to have a second cleaver, of stainless steel, with a blade 8 inches long by 3¼ inches wide, and of much lighter weight. It is perfect for slicing and its blade is quite useful for pressing out various dumpling skins.

Bamboo Chopsticks.

These are available in packages of 10 pair. Chopsticks are useful not only to dine with, but as mixers, stirrers, and servers.

Chinese Strainer.

A circular steel-mesh strainer attached to a long bamboo handle, these come in many sizes, but for general purposes I prefer one 10 inches in diameter.

A Chinese strainer

Strainer.

A fine all-purpose household strainer.

Rolling Pin.

Invest in a heavy hardwood roller.

Broom Handle.

A section of standard broom handle, about 8 inches long, makes a fine ancillary rolling pin for lighter work.

Dough Scraper.

The standard kind used in ordinary baking.

Other Utensils.

In addition to the somewhat specialized utensils listed above, you will need the following to prepare dim sum:

cutting board
wood spoons
small utility knife
pie plate
selection of heatproof dishes
china dishes
square or round cake pans, 8 or 9 inches across
cookie sheets
fluted, scallop-edged custard tins, 3¼ inches diameter
frying pan, cast iron, 10-inches diameter
griddle, nonstick, coated, 8 to 10 inches diameter
hand graters, large and small
masher
garlic press
cookie cutter, round, 4-inch diameter
kitchen shears
rubber spatula

pastry brush
small, fine-point, artist's brush
cooking thermometer, special for deep-frying
ruler
kitchen scale
electric mixer with dough hook (see note)
food processor (see note)

NOTE: Most kitchens these days contain heavy-duty electric mixers equipped with dough hooks. Such an appliance is desirable, particularly for making many of the doughs for dim sum. However, all of the doughs can be kneaded by hand.

A food processor is another option. I use it only sparingly in dim sum cookery, mainly to mash difficult dumpling fillings such as lotus seeds and red beans. A processor is not necessary for the recipes in this book.

厨藝 The Techniques

I have heard repeatedly, from many people, that although they love Chinese food the very idea of preparing it in their own kitchens frightens them. And why? Because, they confess, the use of the somewhat alien wok and cleaver is mysterious, because of what they have heard about the tediousness of hours of cutting and slicing simply so something can be cooked in a very few minutes. They'd rather enjoy it in restaurants, they feel.

Well, on one level they are correct. Fine Chinese food of all schools and regions and of all varieties *can* be enjoyed in today's sophisticated restaurants. On another level they are *so* wrong. Not to cook Chinese food—surely one of the most creative and varied cuisines in the world—at home is to cheat yourself out of the unbelievable satisfaction and well-being that comes with creation. Chinese cuisine, perhaps more than any other, is constantly changing, being added to, altered by the creativeness of its practitioners.

There really is no mystery; there is only learning. Any feelings of mystery vanish once you learn how, and learning the techniques of Chinese cuisine—in our particular case, the ways of dim sum and the teahouse—will be anything but tedious. What you will find instead is delight at the end of the learning.

Tedious?

It seems to me that a couple of hours spent to prepare something that will be both beautiful to contemplate and delicious to taste is not tedium.

34

And when what you have created brings a certain joy, and smiles of satisfaction to the faces of those who are enjoying your efforts, is that not a wonderful reward? I think it is.

This is the sort of feeling I have tried to impart to my students through the years. It is not just biting into tea-smoked duck, for example, that is delicious. The process itself should be delicious; the preparation, the different aromas of anise, cinnamon, scallions, and ginger, the smokiness of Dragon Well tea as the duck is suffused by it—these are as wonderful as the taste of the finished dish.

The key to such enjoyment is, of course, to do things correctly and with economy. If you do not prepare your ingredients and utensils properly then *any* cookery will become overpowering and frustrating—Chinese cuisine perhaps more so because it demands a certain discipline. Yet Chinese cooking generally, and dim sum cooking in particular, can be free of any concerns if you tend to basics.

"Basics" means not only becoming familiar with initially strange food-stuffs and spices, but learning the techniques to be used in dealing with them as well as the properties and capacities of the tools necessary to work with them.

Cooking with the Wok

In a cuisine so steeped in tradition as is Chinese, there is nothing more traditional than the wok. It is a thousand-year-old Chinese creation, first made of iron, later of carbon steel, still later of aluminum, shaped like an oversize soup plate. Its concave shape, which places its belly right into a flame or heat source, makes it an all-purpose cooker ideal for light stir-frying, for pan-frying, deep-frying, and steaming. It is a perfect vessel in which to make sauces as well.

It is, in carbon steel, about as close to perfection as you can get in a cooking utensil. Though it is neither a pot nor a pan, it functions as both. Its shape permits foods to be tossed rapidly through the hot oil in its well without becoming greasy. That same shape permits creation of a large steamer simply by using a cover or tiers of bamboo steamers. Much of the attraction for the wok these days is derived from the realization that wok cooking is natural cooking.

If you buy one wok it should be made of carbon steel. Though not at all pretty when it is new, because of its coating of heavy, sticky oil, the carbon-steel wok, cleaned and seasoned, is ideal and will last for years. It comes in various sizes, but for our purposes a wok 14 inches in diameter will be perfect.

Once bought, it should be washed in extremely hot water with a bit of liquid detergent. The inside should be cleaned with a sponge, the outside with steel wool and cleanser; then it should be rinsed and, still wet, placed over a flame and dried with a paper towel to prevent instant rust. With the wok still over a burner, 1 teaspoon of peanut oil should be tipped into the bowl and rubbed around with a paper towel. This oiling should be repeated until the towel is free of any traces of black residue. Your wok is then ready.

What I usually do with a new wok is make a batch of French-fried potatoes as a first cooking task. That is the perfect way to season a wok. I put in 4 cups of peanut oil, heat it until I see wisps of white smoke rising, then put the potatoes in.

A wok brush

NOTE: After that first washing of your new wok, detergents should *never* be used in the bowl of the wok. It should be washed with extremely hot water, perhaps with a stiff wok brush (inexpensive and usually available where you buy your wok) or a sponge. After rinsing, it should be dried quickly with a paper towel, then placed over a flame for thorough drying. If you have finished cooking in it for the day, then it should be reseasoned with a bit of peanut oil rubbed around the inside with a paper towel. This should be done for at least the first 15 or 20 uses of the wok until it becomes shiny and dark-colored, which indicates that it is completely seasoned.

If the wok is to be used several times in the course of one cooking session, then it should be washed, wiped with a towel, and dried over heat after each use.

The carbon-steel spatula you use with your wok requires the same care.

The wok is indispensable for dim sum cookery. All of its capabilities are utilized: it is used to stir-fry the various dim sum fillings; to deep-fry such delicacies as spring rolls, shrimp toasts, and stuffed crab claws; to oil-blanch vegetables and meats so they retain their flavor and juices; to water-blanch, which effectively removes water from vegetables and meats; and finally, for steaming—which is truly the cornerstone of dim sum cooking.

Stir-frying

Stir-Frying.

This is by far the most dramatic of Chinese cooking techniques. It is fascinating to watch finely sliced and chopped food being whisked through a touch of oil and tossed from the wok with a spatula. Hands and arms move, the wok is often tipped back and forth. Stir-frying seems to be all movement. But mostly it is preparation.

The object of stir-frying is to cook vegetables exactly to the point at which they retain their flavor, color, crispness, and nutrition. Meat is generally shredded or thinly sliced and seared so that its juices are kept in. To do this you must prepare all of the elements of your dish before stir-frying.

All vegetables, for example, thinly and evenly cut, must be next to the wok, ready to be tipped into the hot oil, and so must the meat and shellfish that are to accompany them. This is simply organization, so that as you cook you will have everything within your reach and the rhythm of stir-frying will not be interrupted. The best stir-fried preparations are those that retain their natural characteristics while at the same time picking up and retaining the heat from the wok.

To stir-fry: Heat the wok for 45 seconds to a minute, pour oil into the wok and coat the sides by spreading oil with a spatula. Drop a slice of ginger in the oil and when it becomes light brown the oil is ready. (When cooking vegetables I usually add a touch of salt to the oil, but not when cooking meat or fish, which usually have been marinated or otherwise preseasoned.) Then place the food in the wok and begin tossing it through the oil, 1 or 2 minutes for such soft vegetables as bean sprouts, bok choy, or scallions, about a minute longer for harder vegetables such as cabbage, carrots, or broccoli. Scoop out the vegetables with a spatula and they are ready to be served.

If vegetables are too wet they will not stir-fry well, so they should be patted dry with paper towels. If they are too dry, however, you may have to sprinkle a few drops of water with your hand into the wok while cooking. When water is sprinkled in this manner bits of steam are created which aid in the cooking process.

Meats and shellfish, particularly shrimp, generally are stir-fried for about 3 to 4 minutes until their color changes.

Stir-frying may appear initially as a rather frenzied activity, but really it isn't and the more you do the more you will realize that it is simply establishing a cooking rhythm.

Deep-fat Frying.

The object of deep-fat frying is to cook food through inside while its outside becomes golden and lightly crusty. Most foods that are to be deep-fried are first seasoned, marinated, dipped in batter, or fashioned into particular shapes, and the object of the deep-frying process is for the oil to combine with these other tastes to create new and fresh flavors.

When I wish to make my wok into a deep-fryer I heat it briefly and then place 4 to 6 cups of peanut oil inside and heat the oil to 325 to 375 degrees Fahrenheit, depending upon what I am cooking.

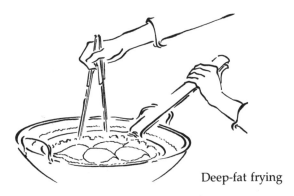

Deep-fat frying

The oil should be heated to a temperature a bit higher than that required for frying the food, because when food is placed in it, the oil temperature will drop. For example, when I wish to deep-fry dumplings at 325 degrees, I heat the oil to 350 degrees, then place the dumplings in. The temperature drops, then rises again, and I use a frying thermometer (which I leave in the oil) to regulate the oil.

Softer dim sum, such as Woo Gok, need oil heated to 350 or 375 degrees; harder dim sum, such as dumplings, cook at from 325 to 350 degrees.

When the oil reaches the proper temperature, slide the food from the inside edge of the wok into the oil. I suggest you cook only 3 or 4 dim sum at a time until you become more expert. Cook them until golden brown and crispy on both sides, turning them over as they cook. They will usually cook thoroughly, and properly, in about 3 to 5 minutes. Remember to keep the temperature of the oil steady by turning the heat up or down as required.

The utensil to use for deep-frying is the Chinese mesh strainer. Its large surface and stout bamboo handle are ideal for removing foods from oil and straining them as well. In my view, this strainer is far more useful than a slotted spoon.

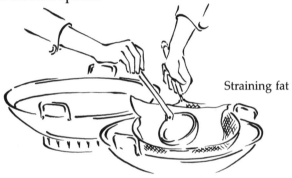

Straining fat

Oil-Blanching.

This relatively simple cooking technique is basically a sealing process. Its aim is to seal in the flavor of vegetables, meats, and shellfish, and to retain the bright color of vegetables.

For vegetables, heat the wok, place 3 cups of peanut oil in it and heat to exactly 300 degrees Fahrenheit. Vegetables should be added to the oil for no longer than 30 to 45 seconds and then removed with a Chinese strainer.

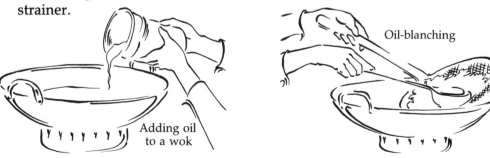

Adding oil to a wok

Oil-blanching

For meats and shellfish, the oil should be at exactly 350 degrees. Food is placed on the mesh of the strainer and then lowered into the oil for about 1 to 1½ minutes.

When foods are removed from the oil, the excess oil should be drained off and the oil-blanched foods set aside to be used as required.

Water-Blanching.

This method removes water from vegetables, meats, and shellfish and makes for lighter dim sum fillings.

For both vegetables and meats, place 3 to 4 cups of water in your wok, add ¼ teaspoon of baking soda to the water, and bring it to a boil.

For vegetables, place in water and bring the water back to a boil. Immediately drain vegetables in a strainer, place them in a bowl, and run cold water over them. Strain again and squeeze out excess water with a piece of cheesecloth. Set aside.

For meats and shellfish: Bring water to a boil. Drop in food and bring back to a boil. Remove and strain, then place the food in a bowl, run cold water over it, and let it stand for 1 minute. Drain and set aside.

The process for water-blanching meat and shellfish is required but once in this dim sum book and then only with a variation. In the preparation of Nor Mai Gai, Stuffed Lotus Leaves, the chicken, pork, and shrimp in the recipe are water-blanched. In this very special instance I add star anise, scallions, and ginger to the water, then I blanch all three in this flavored water. The water is discarded after the blanching, but cold water is *not* run over the water-blanched foods, so that the added flavor will not be dissipated.

Water-blanching

Adding water
to a wok

Steaming.

Chinese-style steaming is almost a life-giving process. Doughs become soft, light, and firm breads, dumplings, and buns when subjected to steam's wet, penetrating heat. Food that is dried becomes moist, that which is shrunken expands. Steaming preserves flavor and bestows, particularly to doughs, a glistening coat.

It is an artful technique as well, because foods can be placed in lovely arrangements within bamboo steamers and, once cooked, they can be served without being disturbed. Steaming requires virtually no oil, except that used to coat the bamboo reeds at the bottom of the steamers to prevent sticking. (Even a bamboo leaf or a lettuce leaf can be used as a liner, thus eliminating any need for oil.)

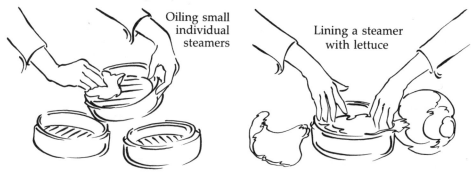

Oiling small individual steamers

Lining a steamer with lettuce

To steam, place 4 to 5 cups of water in a wok and bring it to a boil. Place steamers in wok so that they sit evenly above, but not touching, the water. Depending upon the number and size of the dim sum to be steamed, you will be able to stack as many as three steamers, covering the top, and the contents of all will cook beautifully.

Most steamed dim sum steam thoroughly in 7 to 12 minutes. Steamed rice requires 25 to 35 minutes. Cakes require from 1 to 1½ hours.

Boiling water should be on hand at all times during the steaming process, to replace any water that evaporates from the wok.

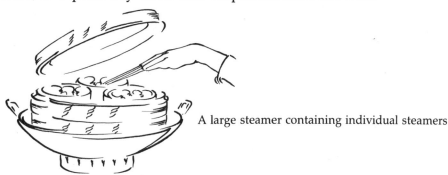

A large steamer containing individual steamers

Preparing porcelain and Pyrex for steaming.

Occasionally dim sum are placed within steamers in porcelain or Pyrex dishes to cook and to serve on. These dishes must first be seasoned, or tempered.

Fill your wok with 5 to 6 cups of cold water. Place a cake rack inside and pile up dishes to be prepared on the rack, making certain they are completely covered by the cold water. Cover with a wok cover and bring the water to a boil. Let the water boil for 10 minutes, turn off heat, and allow the wok to cool to room temperature. The dishes are then seasoned and can be placed in steamers without fear that they will crack.

Working with the Cleaver

If the wok is an all-purpose cooker then the cleaver comes close to being the perfect all-purpose cutting instrument. The Chinese kitchen would not be a kitchen without the broad-bladed, wood-handled cleaver, and nobody who cooks Chinese food should be without one. Rather formidable-looking, the cleaver occasionally frightens people who think that the first time they use it they will slice off one or more of their fingers. This is, of course, nonsense.

The cleaver, when held correctly, so that its weight and balance will be well utilized, can do virtually anything a handful of lesser knives can. It slices, shreds, threads, dices, chops, and hacks, all with great ease. It mashes, it is a scoop, it can function as a dough scraper, and it even serves as a work surface for a limited number of dim sum.

Cleavers come in various sizes and weights, some about $3/4$ of a pound, which are fine for slicing and cutting, heavier sorts of about 1 pound which are better for mincing, and still heavier cleavers of about 2 pounds that will chop through any meat and all but the heaviest bones. If you are to have but a single all-purpose cleaver, I recommend one that weighs about 1 pound, is about 8 inches long, and has a blade $3^{1}/_{2}$ to $3^{3}/_{4}$ inches wide.

Different people hold cleavers in different ways, and much is made of the "proper" way to hold one—but there really is no single way to hold a cleaver. However, it should be held comfortably and in such a way as to make the weight of the blade do its work efficiently and firmly.

I use two basic grips.

The first, for chopping and mincing: I grip the handle in a fistlike grasp and swing it straight down. The stroke will be long and forceful if I am cutting bone or something quite thick. If I am mincing, the strokes will be short, rapid, and controlled. The wrist dictates the force.

The second, for slicing, shredding, and dicing: I grip the handle as before, but permit the index finger to stretch out along the side of the flat blade to give it guidance. The wrist, which barely moves with this grip, is virtually rigid and almost becomes an extension of the cleaver, as the blade is drawn across the food to be cut. When you use this grip, your other hand becomes a guide. Your fingertips should anchor the food to be cut and your knuckle joints should guide the cleaver blade, which will brush them ever so slightly as it moves across the food.

In most dim sum preparations vegetables and meats are sliced, shredded, or diced. Garlic, occasionally ginger, and shrimp are generally minced.

A cleaver, because it is made of carbon steel, should be washed and dried quickly to prevent rust. Under no circumstances should it be placed in a dishwasher. If your cleaver should show a spot of rust, it should be rubbed off with steel wool, dried, and touched with a bit of vegetable oil.

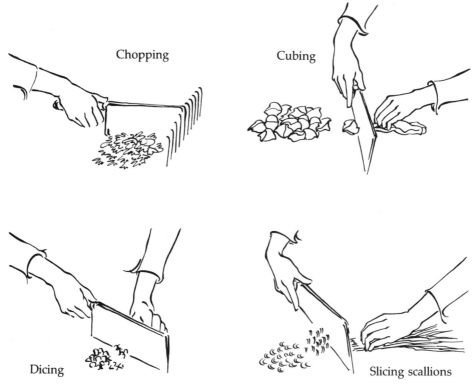

Chopping

Cubing

Dicing

Slicing scallions

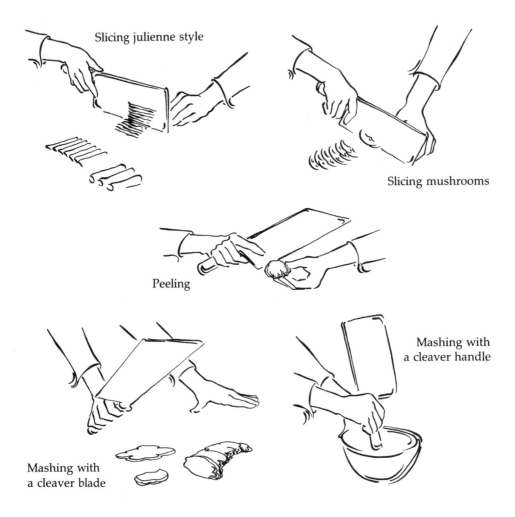

Slicing julienne style

Slicing mushrooms

Peeling

Mashing with
a cleaver handle

Mashing with
a cleaver blade

Eating in the Chinese Manner

Dim sum is the most informal of meals, served randomly, its dishes set out in no particular order except at the whim of those eating. Just about the only rule is to eat sweets toward the end of the meal, but even that is a rule to be broken.

Dim sum can, however, be served formally, in individual porcelain dishes, or family-style out of large platters or steamers. How you serve depends upon your taste and inclinations.

There is, of course, only *one* way to hold chopsticks properly:

Just as there is a proper way to hold a rice bowl or soup bowl, and those small Chinese spoons:

It now becomes time to cook, to eat, and to enjoy.

The Chinese way
to hold chopsticks

The Chinese way
to eat with chopsticks

The proper way to hold
a Chinese soup spoon

The correct way to hold a
Chinese soup bowl and spoon

The Dim Sum Recipes

點心食譜

Wheat Starch—Tapioca Flour Dough

HAR GAU	*Shrimp Dumplings*
FUNG NGAN GAU	*Phoenix Eyes*
FUN GUOR	*Rice Noodle Fruit*
JAI GAU	*Vegetarian Dumplings*

Basic Wheat Flour—Siu Mai Dough

SOI GAU	*Water Dumplings*
SIU MAI	*Cook and Sell Dumplings*

Steamed Bun Dough
Steamed Bun Dough (from Starter)

CHAR SIU	*Roast Pork*
JING CHAR SIU BAU	*Steamed Pork Buns*
LOP CHEUNG GUEN	*Steamed Sausage Buns*
NOR MAI GUEN	*Glutinous Rice Loaf*
GUK CHAR SIU BAU	*Baked Pork Buns*

Pastry Dough

DAU SAH SO BANG	*Red Bean Paste Pastry*
LOR BOK SO BANG	*Turnip Pastry*
GAH LI GAI SO BANG	*Curried Chicken Pastry*
CHUNG YAU BANG	*Scallion Pancakes*
FU LIT YAU BANG	*Fred's Special Scallion Pancakes*
GAU JI	*Shanghai Dumplings or Little Dumplings*
SIU LOON BAU	*Soup Dumplings*
DAI GUT YAU GOK	*Good Luck Dumplings*

麵團 Dumplings and Other Doughs

The many doughs of dim sum and their changing consistencies and properties comprise perhaps the most important and intriguing aspect of dim sum cookery. Most dim sum are dumplings, buns, or breads based on white doughs—the majority made of wheat flour, some made of glutinous rice flour, and a very few made of rice flour. All flours are called "fun," or powder, by the Chinese, so that wheat flour is *mien fun*, a high-gluten wheat flour or noodle flour is *gun mien fun*, glutinous rice flour is *nor mai fun*, and rice flour is *jim mai fun*.

All of these flours are pure white and this aspect is most pleasing to the Chinese, for whom the appearance of dim sum is as important as the taste. Dim sum, for them, must be white, and the whiter the flour the whiter the steamed or baked dough will be.

White flour is simply the end product of the milling process. It is the most commonly used flour and comes from the wheat kernel, which also includes the coarse outer layer called bran, the oily germ, and the starchy core called the endosperm. The bran and germ contain most of wheat's vitamins and minerals, but because they spoil rather quickly and make for a rough-textured product, these are discarded in the milling of fine white flour. Since this flour contains only the endosperm, which has few vitamins or minerals, it is "enriched" with additions of iron, thiamine, riboflavin, and niacin.

The gluten portion of flour, actually its protein component, is what gives elasticity to doughs. The more gluten in the flour, the more elastic

49

the dough and the greater its strength. Gluten is often added to white flour too, in the form of gluten flour. This is manufactured by preparing a dough from regular wheat flour, washing away its starch-laden portion, drying what is left, and then grinding it fine. The protein content of white flour is usually about 10 percent; with gluten flour added, this rises to about 12 percent. But more important, the addition of gluten makes regular white flour more elastic.

In general, flour is milled especially for dim sum and is sold to dim sum restaurants in 100-pound bags. Obviously it cannot be expected that you or I will buy flour in such vast quantities. So what I have done is to experiment meticulously with flours readily available on market shelves, flours available in quantities as small as 2-pound sacks.

You will see various legends on flour bag labels. Let me help you decipher them.

All-Purpose Flour: One composed of half hard wheat with gluten for tensile strength, one-half soft wheat that is better-quality flour.

Enriched Flour: Flour with added nutrition.

Bread Flour: Usually flour with high gluten content.

Bromated Flour: A combination of wheat flour and malted barley flour.

Short Patent: White flour, often made whiter by gas.

Standard Patent: Less white.

For purposes of dim sum cookery, the important characteristics of flour are that it is white, has a high proportion of gluten, and contains hard wheat for strength. I have already listed the wheat flours that have proved to be most dependable under all cooking and climate conditions, and the recipes indicate which of these flours I prefer to use in order to make the finest of that particular dim sum.

Other flours or powders are sometimes added to white flour doughs. The most common are tapioca powder, ground from the root of the cassava, and glutinous rice powder, which is ground from dry glutinous rice. Both add tensile strength to their doughs.

WHEAT STARCH — TAPIOCA FLOUR DOUGH

This dough, based on a combination of wheat starch and tapioca flour, is one of the most traditional doughs used in dim sum preparation.

Dumplings made with it can have a variety of fillings. I use this dough for several Cantonese dim sum:

HAR GAU   *(Shrimp Dumplings), page 52*
FUNG NGAN GAU   *(Phoenix Eyes), page 54*
FUN GUOR   *(Rice Noodle Fruit), page 56*
JAI GAU   *(Vegetarian Dumplings), page 57*

The small individual pieces of dough, when formed into thin dim sum wrappings, are called *pei*, meaning "skin."

   2 cups wheat starch
   1 cup tapioca flour
 ½ teaspoon salt
1¾ cups boiling water
   3 tablespoons lard
 ½ teaspoon sesame oil

1.   In the bowl of an electric mixer, place the wheat starch, the tapioca flour, and the salt. Start the mixer, and as the bowl and dough hook rotate, add boiling water. (If electric mixer is unavailable, hand mix in same order, pouring boiling water with one hand while mixing with a wooden spoon with the other hand.)
2.   Add the lard and the sesame oil and mix together thoroughly. (You may have to assist mixing process with rubber spatula.) If dough is too dry, add 1 teaspoon of water.
3.   Continue mixing until a ball of dough forms. Remove from bowl, knead a few times, divide into four equal pieces, place each ball in plastic bag to retain moisture until ready to use.

   To form the skin
1.   Before working with dough, oil the work surface. Soak a paper towel in oil and repeatedly rub cleaver across folded towel so that cleaver blade is slightly oiled.
2.   Roll pieces of dough into sausage-shaped lengths about 12 inches

long and 1 inch in diameter. Cut a ¹/₂-inch piece from the length. Roll into a small ball, then press down with the palm of your hand.

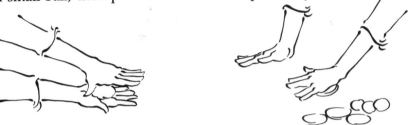

3.   Press flat with the broad side of the cleaver to create the round skin, 2¹/₄ inches in diameter.

NOTE: Dough can be set aside for a few hours, or overnight in cold weather. It must remain at room temperature; it cannot be refrigerated or frozen.

   If your electric mixer does not have a dough hook, you must mix the dough by hand. You cannot use a hand mixer with beaters.

HAR GAU
Shrimp Dumplings
70 dumplings

Har gau is the most famous dim sum in Canton. It is light and delicate and favored by young and old. Chinese children regard har gau with the same reverence that American children give to hamburgers, and in the teahouse it is always the dim sum that is first to sell out.

   2¹/₂ tablespoons fresh pork fat, either bought packaged or trimmed
         from a fresh ham or from pork chops
   ³/₄ pound shrimp, shelled, deveined, washed, dried, and diced

1 teaspoon salt
1½ teaspoons sugar
½ egg white, beaten
1½ tablespoons tapioca flour
2 teaspoons oyster sauce
1 teaspoon sesame oil
   Pinch of white pepper
⅓ cup water chestnuts, diced
⅓ cup white portion of scallions, finely chopped
¼ cup bamboo shoots, diced
1 Wheat Starch—Tapioca Flour Dough recipe, *page 50*

1.   Drop pork fat into 1½ cups boiling water and allow to boil until it cooks fully and becomes translucent. Remove from water, place in bowl, run cold water over it, let stand for several minutes, remove from water, dry with paper towel, and dice.
2.   Place shrimp in bowl of electric mixer. Start mixer and add, mixing thoroughly between each addition, the salt, sugar, egg white, tapioca flour, oyster sauce, sesame oil, and white pepper.
3.   Add cooked pork fat, water chestnuts, scallions, and bamboo shoots. Combine evenly and thoroughly.
4.   Remove the mixture from the mixing bowl and place it in a shallow bowl or dish and refrigerate for 4 hours or put it in the freezer for 25 minutes.
5.   Using Wheat Starch—Tapioca Flour Dough skins, form the dumplings: Place ½ teaspoon of shrimp filling into the center of each skin, then fold the skin in half, forming a crescent or half-moon shape.

6.   Hold the dumpling securely in your left hand, then begin to form the pleats with the fingers of your right hand. Continue to form small pleats until the dumpling is completely closed.

7.   Press the top edge of the dumpling between your thumb and index fingers to seal it tightly. Tap the sealed edge lightly with your knuckle to give the dumpling its final shape.

8.   Steam for 5 to 7 minutes and serve immediately.

❧Har Gau can be frozen for future use. They keep for at least 3 months when piled neatly and wrapped in a double layer of plastic wrap and then in foil.
   To reheat, defrost, then steam for 3 to 5 minutes.

 F U N G   N G A N   G A U
Phoenix Eyes
70 dumplings

 The phoenix is the traditional symbol of the bride or the woman of nobility and, quite simply, these dumplings, called "phoenix eyes," are shaped to look like women's eyes.

1½ pounds shrimp, shelled, deveined, washed, dried, and quartered
   1 to 1½ teaspoons salt, to taste
   1 egg white, beaten
2½ tablespoons tapioca flour
2½ teaspoons sugar
2½ tablespoons boiled pork fat, diced (see Har Gau, *page 52*)
   1 teaspoon sesame oil
   1 tablespoon oyster sauce
      Pinch of white pepper
¼ cup white portion of scallions, finely chopped
   1 Wheat Starch—Tapioca Flour Dough recipe, *page 50*

1.   Place shrimp in bowl of electric mixer. Add salt and blend for 5 minutes.

2.   Add egg white and blend for 2 minutes.

3.   Add tapioca flour and blend for 1 minute.

4.   Add sugar, pork fat, sesame oil, oyster sauce, white pepper, and scallions and blend thoroughly for 5 to 7 minutes.

5.   Using Wheat Starch—Tapioca Flour dough, form dumpling wrapping. (These wrappings should be slightly thicker than wrappings for Har Gau or Fun Guor.)

6.   Place 2 teaspoons of filling in center of each wrapping. Fold the skin in half to form a crescent shape. With your index fingers, create a pleat on each side of the dumpling. Press and seal the side edges of the dumpling to form the Phoenix Eye shape.

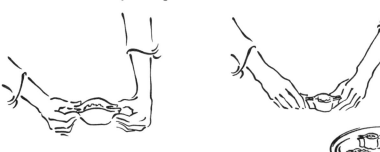

7.   Steam for 5 to 7 minutes and serve immediately.

✄ Fung Ngan Gau may be frozen and will keep for about 3 months. To freeze, wrap in a double layer of plastic wrap and cover with foil.

To reheat, defrost thoroughly and steam for 3 to 5 minutes.

F U N   G U O R
Rice Noodle Fruit
70 to 80 dumplings

I am often asked why these are called "rice noodle fruit" and my reply is that I really do not know. Perhaps it is because its half-moon shape looks like a slice of apple or a wedge of orange? Perhaps.

2 tablespoons liquefied pork fat or peanut oil
1 pound coarsely ground pork, to which add 1½ teaspoons tapioca flour, mixing well
6 ounces shrimp, shelled, deveined, washed, dried, and cut into ⅛-inch dice
⅓ cup Chinese mushrooms, soaked, diced into ⅛-inch pieces
¾ cup winter bamboo shoots, diced into ⅛-inch pieces
2 tablespoons white wine

Combine in bowl and set aside:
    1¼ teaspoons salt
    2¼ teaspoons sugar
    1 teaspoon sesame oil
    1 to 2 teaspoons light soy sauce
    3 tablespoons tapioca flour
    4 tablespoons cornstarch
    2 tablespoons oyster sauce
    Pinch of white pepper
    1½ cups chicken broth or chicken soup

3 to 4 tablespoons coriander, finely chopped
1 Wheat Starch—Tapioca Flour Dough recipe, *page 50*

1.   Heat wok. Using liquefied pork fat or peanut oil, stir-fry ground pork, shrimp, mushrooms, and bamboo shoots until pork turns dark and shrimp turns pink.
2.   To the wok, add wine and ingredients from bowl. Cook until sauce thickens and turns dark brown, then add coriander. Remove from wok, place in shallow baking dish, and refrigerate uncovered overnight.
3.   Using Wheat Starch—Tapioca Flour dough, make dim sum wrappings.
4.   Place 1 to 1½ teaspoons filling in center and fold wrapping into half-moon shape. Squeeze edges to seal.

5.   Steam 4 to 6 minutes. Serve immediately.

❧Fun Guor can be frozen but will keep for only about 4 weeks. Wrap in a double layer of plastic wrap and cover with foil.
      To reheat, defrost thoroughly and steam for 3 to 5 minutes.

J A I   G A U
Vegetarian Dumplings
60 to 70 dumplings

The Chinese, as I have noted before, are a most practical people. Years ago, vegetarian dumplings were virtually unknown and strict vegetarians were few. Now, because there are more vegetarians, I've included this vegetarian dumpling, which is perfect for them.

3 cups peanut oil (to blanch vegetables)

Wash, dry thoroughly, shred, and set aside:
      1 cup snow peas
      1 cup carrots
      1 cup celery
      1 cup bamboo shoots
      4 fresh water chestnuts
      12 Chinese dried mushrooms, soaked to soften

1/2 tablespoon peanut oil

In a small bowl, combine to make a sauce:
      2 tablespoons oyster sauce
      1 1/2 teaspoons dark soy sauce
      2 1/2 tablespoons tapioca flour
      1 1/2 teaspoons salt
      2 teaspoons sugar
      1 1/2 teaspoons sesame oil
         Pinch of white pepper
      4 tablespoons cold water

1 Wheat Starch—Tapioca Flour Dough recipe, *page 50*

1.   Heat wok. Add the 3 cups of peanut oil, and heat to 325° to 350°F. Put the vegetables in the hot oil and blanch for about 30 to 40 seconds. Remove the vegetables from the oil and drain them in a strainer. Set the vegetables aside.

2.   Pour the excess oil from the wok into a can to reserve for another use. Wipe wok, then in it heat 1/2 teaspoon of peanut oil. Add the combined sauce ingredients from the small bowl, and cook until the sauce thickens and turns a dark brown.

3.   Place the vegetables in the bowl of an electric mixer. Start mixer, add sauce from wok, and blend thoroughly.

4.   Remove vegetable-sauce mixture, place in a shallow baking dish, and refrigerate for at least 4 hours or overnight.

5.   Follow steps 3, 4, and 5 from Fun Guor recipe, *page 56.*

✂━Vegetarian Dumplings cannot be frozen.

BASIC WHEAT FLOUR— SIU MAI DOUGH
100 squares

These dough squares can be bought as "won ton" skins, which is the Americanization of "wan tun." They come in 1-pound packages, usually 90 to 100 skins to the pound, and in varying thicknesses. I prefer the thinner ones, and because of this I recommend that you buy the skins since commercial dough makers can make them far thinner than you will be able to do in your home. Nevertheless, if you do not have access to a Chinese market or a food outlet that sells won ton skins, here is a recipe for the dough.

   3 cups of flour, Pillsbury Bleached
   1 teaspoon baking soda
   4 extra large eggs
   1/4 cup water
   1/2 cup cornstarch, for dusting

1.   Place the flour mixed with baking soda on work surface. Make a well

in the center and add the eggs. Work the dough with your fingers until all of the egg is absorbed. Slowly dribble in the water, mixing as you do, until the dough is thoroughly mixed. Use a scraper to pick up excess dough. Begin to knead.

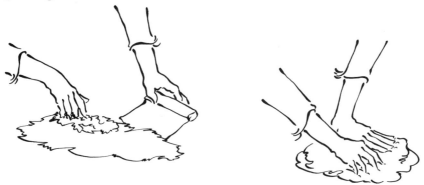

2.   Knead the dough for 10 minutes or until it becomes elastic. Set aside, covered with a damp cloth, for 6 hours.
3.   When the dough is ready, dust the work surface with cornstarch. Roll out the dough with a rolling pin until you have a sheet that is 1/4 inch thick.
4.   Pick up the sheet and dust the work surface again with cornstarch. Continue rolling out until the dough reaches an overall thickness of 1/8 inch.
5.   Roll up the dough around a long piece of broom handle or dowling. Dust the work surface again. Roll the dough out with the pin, as thinly as possible, then roll the dough around broom handle again. (You must pick up the dough by rolling it around the broom handle. Otherwise, it will tear.)
6.   Dust the work surface yet again, unroll the sheet onto surface and with rolling pin roll out a sheet about 22 by 20 inches.
7.   Before cutting, be certain to dust the work surface again with cornstarch. Using the edge of a dough scraper to cut, and the edge of a rule to measure and guide, cut squares 2 3/4 by 2 3/4 inches.

NOTE: The skins will be more elastic if made, then stored overnight in the refrigerator after being wrapped in plastic wrap.

✄ The skins can be frozen for 1 to 2 months.

SOI GAU
Water Dumplings
70 to 80 dumplings

These are very aptly called "water dumplings" because they are either completely or partly cooked in boiling water, and the cooking process is finished in tiny individual servers.

    1 pound fresh pork, ground
 1/4 pound shrimp, shelled, deveined, washed, dried, and cut into 1/8-inch dice
 1/3 cup bamboo shoots, cut into 1/8-inch dice
 1/3 cup fresh water chestnuts, peeled, washed, dried, and cut into 1/8-inch dice
 1/3 cup white portion of scallions, finely chopped
    2 tablespoons boiled pork fat, cut into 1/8-inch dice (see Har Gau, *page 52*)
    1 to 2 tablespoons coriander, to taste, finely chopped
 2 1/4 teaspoons salt
 3 1/4 teaspoons sugar
 1 1/2 teaspoons sesame oil
      Pinch of white pepper
    2 tablespoons tapioca flour
    1 egg, beaten
    1 Basic Wheat Flour—Siu Mai Dough recipe, *page 58*, or 70 to 80 won ton skins

1.   In the bowl of an electric mixer, combine all ingredients except won ton skins and beaten egg. Blend evenly and thoroughly; refrigerate for 4 hours.
2.   Using kitchen scissors, cut won ton skins into circular pieces 2 1/4 inches in diameter.

3.   Place 1½ to 2 teaspoons of filling in center of each skin. With a butter knife, brush egg around the outer edge of the skin. Fold skin into half-moon shape and press together tightly with thumb and forefinger to seal.
4.   Cook dumplings in 3 quarts of boiling water for 5 to 7 minutes. Run cold water over cooked dumplings and drain. Serve immediately.

❧ Soi Gau can be kept refrigerated for about 7 days or frozen for about 3 months. If you plan to freeze them for future use, undercook them by 2 minutes, drain, and dry them before freezing. To recook, defrost thoroughly, then steam them for 3 to 4 minutes.

Won ton skins come in 1-pound packages, containing usually 100 or more pieces. Those not needed for this recipe can be frozen for future use.

S I U   M A I
Cook and Sell Dumplings
45 to 50 dumplings

These dim sum bear the delightful description "cook and sell," simply because they are shaped like tiny cooking kettles, kettles full of food. And because they are so tasty and so pretty they are never left unsold.

12 Chinese dried mushrooms, soaked for ½ hour in hot water,
        rinsed, dried, stems discarded, caps diced into ¼-inch pieces
 1 pound pork butt, coarsely ground
½ pound shrimp, shelled, deveined, washed, dried, and diced into
        ¼-inch pieces
1½ teaspoons salt
 2 teaspoons sugar
1½ tablespoons peanut oil
 2 tablespoons cornstarch
 1 teaspoon sesame oil
½ teaspoon peanut butter
   Pinch of white pepper
 1 Basic Wheat Flour—Siu Mai Dough recipe, *page 58,* or 45 to 50
        won ton skins

1.   Combine all ingredients (except won ton skins) in electric mixer and mix until consistency is smooth and even. Refrigerate for 4 hours.

2.   Using kitchen scissors, cut won ton skins into rounds, 2¼ inches in diameter.

3.   Into the middle of each round, place 1 tablespoon of filling. Holding the filling in place with the blade of a small rounded knife in one hand, and holding dumpling in the other hand, gradually turn knife and dumpling slowly in the same direction, so dumpling forms a basket shape.

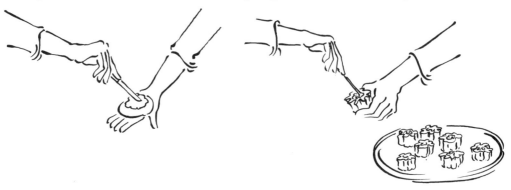

4.   Remove the knife, pack down and smooth the filling on top of dumpling. Squeeze the dumpling to create a neck so that the dumpling and filling will remain intact during the steaming process. Tap dumpling lightly on the work surface to flatten the bottom so that it will stand upright in the steamer.

5.   Steam for 5 to 7 minutes. Serve immediately.

✄ Siu Mai can be frozen either before or after steaming. They will keep 2 to 3 months. To reheat, defrost thoroughly and steam for 3 to 5 minutes.

Since a 1-pound package of won ton skins contains 100 or more skins, half a package can be frozen to prepare a future Siu Mai recipe.

STEAMED BUN DOUGH

This dough, with a bleached-flour base, is ideal for several steamed varieties of dim sum, particularly jing char siu bau, those roast-pork-filled buns that become flowerlike as they steam. Once this dough has cooked through, it becomes soft and spongelike and complements its various fillings such as roast pork, lotus seed paste, red bean paste, and lop cheung—cured

Chinese sausage. It is also fine for a strudellike roll when it is filled with a glutinous rice mixture.

2¼ cups flour
3½ teaspoons baking powder
  ½ cup sugar
   3 ounces milk
1½ ounces water
   2 tablespoons lard

1.   Mix flour, baking powder, and sugar together on work surface; then make a well in the middle.

2.   Add milk gradually and with fingers combine it with flour mixture.
3.   After milk has been absorbed, add water and with fingers continue to work the dough.
4.   Add lard, and, again with fingers, continue to work dough.
5.   Using a dough scraper, gather the dough with one hand and begin kneading with the other hand.
6.   Knead for 12 to 15 minutes. If the dough is dry, add 1 teaspoon of water at a time and continue to knead, until the dough becomes elastic. If the dough is wet, sprinkle a bit of flour on the work surface and on your hands and continue working.
7.   When dough is elastic, cover with moderately damp cloth and allow dough to rest for about 1 hour.

NOTE: Gold Medal All-Purpose Enriched Bleached flour is the best American flour for this recipe. Bleached flour must be used to ensure the snowy white color.

✄ This dough must be used within 1 to 2 hours of the time it has been made. It cannot be frozen.

STEAMED BUN DOUGH (*from Starter*)

If steamed bun dough is *not* used the same day it is made, it becomes starter and can be used as the base for another Steamed Bun Dough recipe. (See Steamed Bun Dough, *page 62*.) As a matter of course, restaurant chefs make extra dough so that they will have starter for the following day. Most of the fine Chinese chefs I know agree that dough made from starter tastes better than that made from scratch.

1. Form a well in the center of *1/2 pound of starter*. Add *1 cup of flour*, *2 1/2 teaspoons baking powder*, and *1/3 cup sugar* and combine with fingers.
2. Add *1 tablespoon hot water* and mix together.
3. Add *2 tablespoons lard* and combine.
4. Knead, following steps 5, 6, and 7 of the basic Steamed Bun Dough recipe, *page 62*.

CHAR SIU
Roast Pork

This filling for both steamed and baked pork buns, as well as for lotus leaf rice, is also called "barbecued pork" by the Cantonese. As a filling, it is particularly pungent and delicious; however, it can be equally tasty by itself—hot, cold, or sliced up and stir-fried with vegetables. I like to call it my "all-purpose pork."

4 1/2 pounds lean pork butt

In a bowl, combine and mix well:
    3 tablespoons dark soy sauce
    3 tablespoons light soy sauce
    3 tablespoons honey
    1/2 teaspoon salt
    3 tablespoons oyster sauce
    2 tablespoons blended whiskey
    3 tablespoons hoisin sauce
    1/8 teaspoon white pepper
    1/2 cake wet preserved bean curd (*see note*)
    1 teaspoon five-spice powder

1.   Cut the pork into strips 1 inch thick. Using a small knife, pierce the meat repeatedly at $1/2$-inch intervals to help tenderize it.
2.   Line a roasting pan with foil. Place the strips of meat in a single layer at the bottom of the roasting pan.
3.   Pour the remaining ingredients from the bowl over the meat, and allow to marinate for 4 hours or overnight.
4.   Preheat the oven to broil. Place the roasting pan inside and roast for 30 to 50 minutes. To test, remove one strip of pork after 30 minutes and slice it to see if it is cooked through. During the cooking period, meat should be basted 5 or 6 times and turned 4 times. If the sauce dries out, add water to the pan.
5.   When the meat is cooked, allow it to cool, then refrigerate it until you are ready to use it.

NOTE: Wet preserved bean curd comes in both cans and jars. The canned bean curds are larger than those that come in jars. If you use the canned curds, only half a cake is required for this recipe; if you use the curds in jars, use 2 small cakes.

✄ Char Siu can be made ahead. It can be refrigerated 4 to 5 days, and it can be frozen for 1 month. Allow it to defrost before using.

JING CHAR SIU BAU
Steamed Pork Buns
16 buns

This is the dim sum that I remember eating the first time my brother took me to a teahouse. Among the Cantonese if you know you are going to a teahouse, then you know you *must* have jing char siu bau.

The filling may be prepared a day ahead of the dough.

1/2 cup onion, diced into 1/4-inch pieces
3/4 cup Roast Pork, cut into 1/2-inch, thinly sliced pieces (see recipe for Roast Pork, *page 64*)
1 tablespoon liquefied pork fat or peanut oil
1 1/2 teaspoons white wine

Combine in bowl:
1 tablespoon oyster sauce
1 1/2 teaspoons dark soy sauce
2 teaspoons ketchup
2 1/4 teaspoons sugar
Pinch of white pepper
2 1/4 teaspoons cornstarch
2 1/2 ounces chicken broth

1/2 teaspoon sesame oil
1 Steamed Bun Dough recipe, *page 62*

To make filling
1. Heat wok for 30 to 40 seconds. Add pork fat or peanut oil and heat until white smoke rises. Add onions and cook over low heat, turning occasionally, until onions turn light brown.
2. Add the roast pork, raise heat, and stir-fry to combine the pork with the onions. Add white wine and mix well.
3. Lower heat and add sauce mixture from bowl. Stir until entire mixture thickens and turns brown.
4. Add sesame oil and mix well.
5. Remove pork mixture from the wok and transfer to a shallow dish. Allow mixture to cool to room temperature, then refrigerate, uncovered, for 4 hours.

To prepare buns

1.   Roll Steamed Bun Dough into a cylindrical piece 16 inches long. Cut into 16 1-inch pieces.

2.   Roll each piece into a ball. Work with one piece at a time; cover those pieces not being used with a damp cloth.

3.   Press ball of dough down lightly; then, working with fingers of both hands, press dough into a domelike shape.

4.   Place 2 tablespoons of filling in center of well that has been created (*see note*). Close and pleat dough with fingers until filling is completely enclosed.

5.   Put buns on squares of wax paper, 2½ by 2½ inches, and place in steamer at least 2 inches apart, to allow for expansion.

6.   Steam for 15 to 20 minutes; serve immediately.

NOTE: Use only 1 tablespoon of filling in the beginning until you have learned to work well with the dough; otherwise, you will have trouble sealing the bun. When you feel comfortable working with the dough, increase the amount of filling to 2 tablespoons.

✂ These may be frozen after cooking and will keep 2 to 3 months. To reheat, defrost thoroughly and steam for 8 to 10 minutes.

LOP CHEUNG GUEN
Steamed Sausage Buns
16 buns

In Canton these steamed sausage buns are a winter treat since the sausage which is at their heart is made only during the cooler winter months. Because we had to wait for them they became doubly a treat for us as youngsters. In the United States, however, there is no need to wait for them.

8 cured Chinese pork sausages (lop cheung)
3 tablespoons oyster sauce
3 tablespoons dark soy sauce
1 tablespoon sesame oil
1 Steamed Bun Dough recipe, *page 62*

1.   Cut sausages in half, lengthwise and diagonally.
2.   In a shallow dish, combine the oyster sauce, soy sauce, and sesame oil. Add the sausage lengths and marinate for 30 minutes.
3.   Roll bun dough into a cylindrical piece 16 inches long. Cut into 16 1-inch pieces. Work with one piece at a time, covering the remaining pieces with a damp cloth to keep them moist.
4.   Roll pieces into sausage shapes 12 inches in length.
5.   Hold the sausage piece by its thinly cut end together with one end of long piece of dough. Press, then wrap the dough around the sausage.

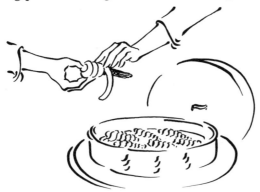

6.   Place sausage rolls on pieces of waxed paper, 3½ by 2 inches. Place in steamer 1 inch apart to allow for expansion.

7. Steam 15 to 20 minutes; serve immediately.

✂These sausage rolls can be frozen after cooking and will keep 2 to 3 months. To reheat, defrost thoroughly and steam for 8 to 10 minutes.

NOR MAI GUEN
Glutinous Rice Loaf
2 loaves

This very rare preparation is still another winter-only treat. After you eat it, you tend to stay quite warm, thus making it not quite the thing to eat if you don't have air-conditioning.

  2 cups glutinous rice (also known as "sweet rice")
  1 tablespoon dried shrimp
  1 teaspoon peanut oil
½ cup Chinese bacon, diced into ¼-inch pieces
  2 cured Chinese sausages (lop cheung), diced into ¼-inch pieces

Combine in bowl:
    2½ tablespoons oyster sauce
      1 teaspoon sugar
      1 teaspoon light soy sauce
      1 teaspoon five-spice powder

⅓ cup scallions, both ends discarded, washed, dried, and thinly
      sliced
½ teaspoon salt (optional)
  1 Steamed Bun Dough recipe, *page 62*

To prepare rice
   Place the rice in large bowl. Wash 3 or 4 times with cold water, then drain thoroughly. Place the rice in a 9-inch cake pan, add 2 cups of cold water, and place the pan in the steamer. Steam for 30 to 40 minutes or until the rice is soft and sticks together. Set aside.

To prepare shrimp

1.   Soak the shrimp in hot water for 1/2 hour, drain thoroughly, and cut into 1/4-inch pieces.
2.   Line a 9-inch square pan with foil and set aside.
3.   In wok, heat 1 teaspoon of peanut oil and stir-fry shrimp for 40 seconds. Add bacon and sausage; stir-fry until meat changes color. Add rice, raise heat, and mix all ingredients well. Lower heat and add sauce mixture from bowl. Stir together thoroughly. Add scallions and mix well. Taste, and, if needed, add 1/2 teaspoon salt and mix very well.
4.   Remove cooked rice mixture from wok and place in foil-lined pan and press down. Press against one side of pan to create a loaf shape 9 inches long, 4 inches wide, and 2 inches high. Allow to return to room temperature, cover loosely with tin foil, and refrigerate for 6 to 8 hours or overnight.
5.   Using a rolling pin, roll out half of the Steamed Bun Dough to make a piece 9 by 9 inches square and 1/4 inch thick. If dough is sticky, dust the work surface and the rolling pin with flour.
6.   Cut filling in half lengthwise. Place half in middle of dough, and trim dough to edges of filling.

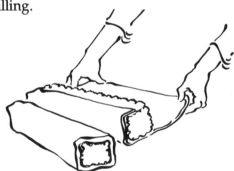

7.   Pick up two ends of dough. Press one end down on filling, overlap with other end, and press down to seal.
8.   Repeat steps 5, 6, and 7 to make the second loaf.
9.   Place loaves on wax paper pieces, 9 by 3 inches. Steam for 15 to 20 minutes. Slice and serve immediately.

NOTE: If some dough is left over after trimming, it may serve as starter.

✄Nor Mai Guen cannot be frozen because the glutinous rice will not retain its cohesion.

GUK CHAR SIU BAU
Baked Pork Buns
12 buns

This is perhaps the most famous dim sum outside of China—that pork-filled baked bun called guk char siu bau. People who are not even familiar with the term "dim sum" know "pork buns," and they are eaten daily by the thousands. Though I have experimented with different fillings for these baked buns, tradition prevails, and roast pork buns remain my favorite.

 1 package dry yeast
 1/3 cup sugar
 1/2 cup hot water
 2 cups high-gluten bread flour
 1/2 egg, beaten
 5 tablespoons lard
 1 recipe Steamed Pork Bun filling, *page 66*

To prepare dough

1. In a large mixing bowl, dissolve the yeast and sugar in hot water. Put in a warm place for 30 to 60 minutes, depending upon the outside temperature. (In the winter, the longer time will be required.)

2. When yeast rises and a brownish foam forms on top, add flour, egg, and lard, stirring continuously with your hand. Begin kneading with your hand.
3. When the mixture becomes cohesive, sprinkle your work surface lightly with flour, place dough on top, and continue kneading. Knead

for about 15 minutes, picking up dough with scraper and sprinkling the work surface with flour to prevent sticking.

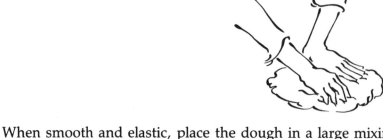

4. When smooth and elastic, place the dough in a large mixing bowl. Cover the bowl with a damp cloth and put it in a warm place to rise. Dough will take from 2 to 4 hours to rise, depending upon temperature (it will take longer in cold weather). The dough is ready when it has tripled in size.

To prepare filling
This filling is identical to that of Jing Char Siu Bau (Steamed Pork Buns). Follow steps 1 through 5 of that recipe.

To prepare buns
1. Preheat oven to 350°F. Cut 12 squares of wax paper, 3½ by 3½ inches.
2. Remove dough from bowl, knead several times, then roll it out with your hands into a roll about 12 inches long. Divide into 12 1-inch pieces. Work with one piece at a time, keeping others under damp cloth.
3. Roll each piece into a ball, then, with fingers, press to create a dome and a well.
4. Place 2 teaspoons of filling into well, hold bun in one hand, and, with the other, turn the bun, pinching it closed. Press firmly to seal.

5.   Place completed bun, sealed-end-down, on square of wax paper. Repeat for other buns.

6.   Place all the buns on a cookie sheet, at least 2 inches apart, to allow for expansion. Put buns in a warm place for about 1 hour to permit them to rise. (The rising time will be longer in winter.)

7.   Using an atomizer, spray each bun lightly with warm water. With a pastry brush, brush each bun with beaten egg.

8.   Bake for 15 to 20 minutes. Halfway through baking time, turn tray around. When the buns are golden brown, remove them from the oven and serve immediately. As the buns cool, the crust will become slightly hard. If you want them to remain soft, brush them lightly with scallion oil, *page 166*, immediately after baking.

NOTE: This recipe uses high-gluten bread flour. I find that Pillsbury's Bread Flour (enriched, bromated, naturally white, high protein, high gluten) works best.

   Use only 1 tablespoon of filling for each bun until you have learned to work well with the dough. Otherwise you will have trouble sealing the bun.

✄These can be frozen after baking. To reheat, defrost and bring to room temperature. Cover with foil and place in a 350°F. oven for 10 to 15 minutes or until hot.

PASTRY DOUGH

This bleached-flour dough is essentially Shanghai in character. It consists of two basic dough mixtures that are combined to give the pastry its flaky texture.

Mixture 1

1½ cups flour (Pillsbury's Best All-Purpose Enriched Bleached is preferred)
  4 ounces plus 1 tablespoon hot water

1.   Place flour on work surface, make a well in center, add hot water slowly, and mix with fingers.
2.   Working with dough scraper, pick up dough and knead for 5 to 7 minutes, until it becomes a cohesive piece and has elasticity. If dough sticks to hands or work surface, sprinkle with flour.
3.   Set dough aside under a damp cloth.

Mixture 2

1½ cups flour (same brand called for above)
8½ tablespoons lard

1.   Place flour on work surface, make a well in center, add lard, and work mixture together with fingers.
2.   Using dough scraper, gather and knead dough, as above. When solid and smoothly soft, set aside in plastic wrap until ready to use.

To prepare pastry
1.   Divide each of the two flour mixtures into 3 equal pieces.

2.   Dust your work surface and rolling pin with flour. Roll 1 piece of mixture 1 into a rectangle about 11 by 6 inches. Place a piece of mixture 2 in the center of the pastry and fold 1 over it.

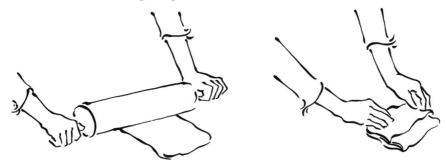

3.   Roll out the dough to a slightly larger rectangle, approximately 12 by 8 inches.

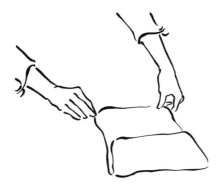

4.   Fold three times and prepare to roll out the dough a third time, following the directions of the specific recipe you are working on. (See Red Bean Paste Pastry, *page 76*; Turnip Pastry, *page 78*; and Curried Chicken Pastry, *page 80*.)

NOTE: All of the fillings and shapes are interchangeable. If you love the chicken filling but prefer a round shape, for example, simply prepare that pastry and that filling.

⊱These two mixtures can be made a day ahead of time and stored in the refrigerator, but mixtures must be at room temperature before combining to make the pastry dough.

DAU SAH SO BANG
Red Bean Paste Pastry
30 pieces

This pastry dim sum is justly famous in Shanghai, as are the two that follow. They are almost unheard of in Canton, and a Cantonese dim sum chef would be bold indeed if he attempted to make these treats from Shanghai.

    1 pound dried red beans
1¼ cups liquefied pork fat or peanut oil
1½ cups dark brown sugar
    1 Pastry Dough recipe, *page 74*
    1 egg, beaten
⅓ cup black sesame seeds
    4 to 5 cups peanut oil

To prepare red bean paste filling

1.   Wash dried beans in a bowl of cold water, discarding any that float. Strain. Place in a bowl with 3 cups cold water and allow to soak for 6 hours.
2.   Put beans and soaking water, plus 2 additional cups of cold water, into a 4-quart pot. Bring to a boil, lower heat, cover, and let beans simmer slowly, stirring from time to time. If water evaporates, add 2 more cups of boiling water. If it evaporates further, add another cup of boiling water.
3.   The beans are cooked when they begin to break apart and all the water dries out. When they are done, place ¼ of the beans in an electric mixer or a food processor with metal blades and mix until a paste forms. Scrape paste into a bowl and repeat this process with each remaining portion of beans.
4.   In wok, heat pork fat or peanut oil. Add sugar and cook until soft. Add bean paste and continue to stir until sugar and beans are thoroughly mashed together. Cook for ½ hour or until mixture becomes very thick and dark brown and purplish in color.
5.   Remove bean mixture from wok, allow to cool, and place in refrigerator for at least 4 hours. Paste must be cool before it can be used for pastry filling.

To prepare pastry

1.   Prepare Pastry Dough recipe, and after folding 3 times (the third rolling of the pastry), roll out to a rectangle 17 by 8 inches.

2.   Roll up dough along its length so piece becomes a 17-inch-long sausage shape. Divide into 10 pieces. Repeat this process with all of the dough (keeping the part not being used under a piece of plastic wrap until ready for use) until you have 30 pieces.

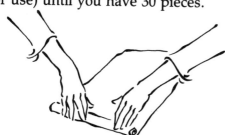 

To form the dumplings

1.   Place 1 small piece of dough on your work surface; press the piece down with your palm. With a small rolling pin, roll it out to make a circular piece 3½ inches in diameter.

2.   In center of dough circle, place 2 teaspoons of bean paste. Gather up sides of dough and, with fingers, turn and crimp it until it is formed into a round shape. Repeat for each of 30 pieces.

3.   Brush egg on sealed side; coat with black sesame seeds. Repeat for all 30 pieces.

4.   In a wok, heat 4 to 5 cups of peanut oil to 300°F. Place pastries, 6 at a time, in oil. Fry until golden brown; remove and serve immediately.

NOTE: If you wish to make this dumpling, but do not want to go to the trouble of making the filling, substitute a 1-pound can of commercial red bean paste.

This recipe yields 4 to 5 cups of bean paste and you will need only 2 cups to make these dumplings. Store the unused bean paste in your refrigerator, where it will keep for about 6 weeks.

⌘These can be frozen after cooking. Reheat in an oven, preheated to between 325° and 350°F., for about 15 to 20 minutes or until hot.

LOR BOK SO BANG
Turnip Pastry

30 pieces

1 pound Chinese turnips (lor bok), peeled, cut into ¾-inch pieces, sliced, and julienned
2 teaspoons salt
4 teaspoons sugar
2 teaspoons sesame oil
4 teaspoons coriander, finely chopped
⅛ teaspoon white pepper
1 Pastry Dough recipe, *page 74*
1 egg, beaten
⅓ cup white sesame seeds
4 to 5 cups peanut oil

1.   In a bowl, combine salt, sugar, sesame oil, coriander, and white pepper. Marinate turnips in this liquid for 6 hours. Drain off liquid and set the turnips aside.

2.   Prepare Pastry Dough, and upon the third rolling out of the pastry (after folding 3 times) roll out the dough to form a 10- by 9-inch rectangle. Roll this up to create a 10-inch-long sausage shape. Cut this into 5 equal pieces.

3.   Split each of these in half lengthwise. Pick up the ends of each piece and fold over and press down. Roll out again with a rolling pin to make a 4- by 4-inch square.

4.   Place 2 teaspoons of drained turnips in the center and, with hands, turn and crimp closed. Remove excess dough. Shape will be rounded but rectangular. Repeat for all 30 pieces.

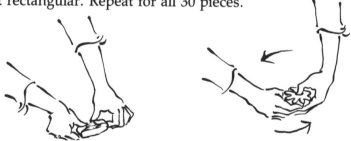

5.   Dip each piece into beaten egg, and coat with white sesame seeds. Repeat for all 30 pastries.

6.   In a wok, heat 4 or 5 cups of peanut oil to 300°F. Place the pastries, 6 at a time, into the oil. Deep-fat fry until golden brown; remove and serve immediately.

❧These cannot be frozen, but they can be kept, after cooking, in the refrigerator for 2 days. To reheat, place the dumplings on a cookie sheet and warm them in a preheated 325° oven for 15 to 20 minutes or until hot.

咖喱鷄酥餅

GAH LI GAI SO BANG
Curried Chicken Pastry
30 pieces

While experimenting with this Shanghai pastry dough and with various fillings, I thought I would try something untraditional, and so I created these curried chicken pastries. The filling complements the flaky pastry very well.

3/4 pound chicken cutlets, cut into 1/4-inch dice

Marinade: in a small bowl, combine:
    1 1/2 teaspoons salt
    2 1/2 teaspoons sugar
    1 1/2 teaspoons sesame oil
    1 1/2 tablespoons oyster sauce
      1 tablespoon cornstarch
    1/8 teaspoon white pepper
    3/4 teaspoon light soy sauce

6 water chestnuts, peeled, washed, dried, and cut into 1/8-inch dice
6 tablespoons celery, cut into 1/8-inch dice
3 teaspoons coriander, finely chopped
3 scallions, finely chopped
2 tablespoons curry powder mixed with 2 tablespoons cold water
3 tablespoons peanut oil or liquefied pork fat
2 cloves garlic, minced
1 1/2 tablespoons white wine

1 or 2 tablespoons chicken broth, if needed
1 Pastry Dough recipe, *page 74*
4 to 5 cups of peanut oil

To prepare filling

1.   Marinate the chicken in the marinade for 1 hour. Set aside.
2.   In a bowl, combine water chestnuts, celery, coriander, and scallions. Set aside. Mix curry powder and water and set aside.
3.   Heat wok; add oil or pork fat. Spread oil over wok's surface, then add minced garlic. When garlic turns brown, add curry-and-water mixture. Raise heat and stir-fry for 1 to 1½ minutes or until the curry releases its fine aroma.
4.   Add chicken with its marinade. Stir. Spread over thin layer; cook for 30 seconds. Turn over and gently mix with the curry.
5.   Add white wine around the edge of the wok. Mix. Add vegetables and stir together. If the mixture is too thick, add 1 or 2 tablespoons of chicken broth. Stir. Remove from wok.
6.   Refrigerate uncovered for at least 4 hours or, preferably, overnight.

To prepare dough

1.   Prepare Pastry Dough, and, on the third rolling out, roll dough into a 10- by 10-inch square. Roll the square into a sausage shape, 10 inches long. Divide into 10 equal pieces.
2.   Press individual pieces down with palm; then, with a small rolling pin, roll each into a circle 3¼ inches in diameter.

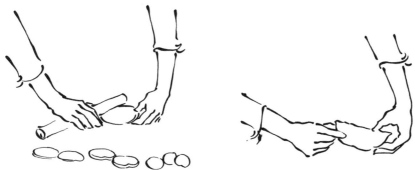

3.   Place 1 tablespoon of curried chicken filling in center of dough circle. Fold into half-moon shape. Holding with one hand, squeeze rim between thumb and forefinger to seal.

4.   With side of thumb, make a decorative scalloped edge. Repeat with all 30 pieces.

5.   In a wok, heat 4 to 5 cups of peanut oil to 300°F. Place the pastries, 6 at a time, into the oil. Deep-fat fry until golden brown. Remove and serve immediately.

✄ These can be frozen after cooking. To reheat, defrost and warm in a 325° to 350°F. oven for 15 to 20 minutes. Or deep fat fry.

CHUNG YAU BANG
Scallion Pancakes
18 to 20 pancakes

Scallion pancakes are a very special Shanghai dim sum. The Cantonese have nothing to compare with it. When the Cantonese talk about dim sum, such delicate preparations as siu mai and har gau come to mind. But to somebody from Shanghai, dim sum is the lusty and rich scallion pancake.

    1 cup vegetable shortening (Crisco preferred)
    3 cups scallions, ends discarded, washed, dried, and chopped finely
1¾ teaspoons salt
1¾ teaspoons sugar
    3 cups flour (Pillsbury's Best All-Purpose Enriched Bleached pre-
       ferred)
    8 ounces hot water (plus another ½ ounce in reserve, if needed)
    8 tablespoons peanut oil, for frying

To prepare filling
In a bowl, combine shortening, scallions, salt, and sugar and mix thoroughly into a paste. Reserve in refrigerator.

To prepare dough
1.   Mound flour onto work surface. Make a well and pour the hot water in with one hand, using fingers of the other hand to mix. When all the water has been poured, knead flour and water into dough. (If dough is too dry, add an extra half ounce of water.)
2.   Using a scraper, pick up the dough and continue to knead for 5 to 7 minutes, until it is smooth and elastic. Cover the dough with a damp cloth and allow it to rest for at least 30 minutes.

To prepare pancakes
1.   Divide the dough into 4 equal pieces. To prevent sticking as you roll out the dough, flour the work surface and rolling pin frequently. Roll each piece into a 12-inch-long roll, 1 inch in diameter.
2.   From the 12-inch roll, cut off a piece 2½ inches long. With rolling pin, roll it out to a piece measuring 10 by 4 inches with rounded edges.

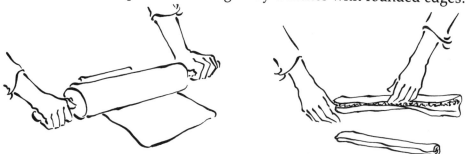

3.   Spread 1½ tablespoons of filling along center of dough.
4.   Fold both sides so that they meet over the filling. Then flatten gently.
5.   Fold in half lengthwise and press again.
6.   Pick up the dough by the ends and gently stretch it, hitting it gently on the work surface at the same time.
7.   Placing the folded edge outward, bring the left end to the middle, creating a circle. Bring the right end around as far as possible to the left. Slip end between folds of dough and press gently. Press gently again so that the roll becomes a solid pancake. Repeat steps 2 through 7 until all the dough is used.

8.   Fry the pancakes in the peanut oil in a heavy skillet, preferably cast iron, until golden brown on both sides. Remove, drain, and serve immediately.

✂—Both the dough and the filling can be made a day ahead of time and refrigerated.

Filling can be frozen and stored for 1 or 2 months.

Cooked Scallion Pancakes can be frozen for 1 to 2 months. To reheat, pan-fry or reheat in 350°F. oven until warmed through.

大葱油餅

FU LIT YAU BANG
Fred's Special Scallion Pancakes
4 pancakes

This large scallion pancake is served most often in restaurants, generally because it requires a bit less effort than the smaller scallion pancakes of the previous recipe. Instead of individual pancakes, this recipe results in 4 pie-sized pancakes that are cut into wedges for serving.

The dough preparation is identical to that for the small scallion pancakes and so is the filling, except for the addition of diced Chinese sausages. The addition of the sausage, which is not traditional, is my husband's suggestion.

    1 cup vegetable shortening (Crisco preferred)
    3 cups scallions, ends discarded, washed, dried, and sliced fine
1¾ teaspoons salt
1¾ teaspoons sugar
    3 cups flour (Pillsbury's Best All-Purpose Enriched Bleached preferred)

8 ounces hot water (plus another ¼ ounce reserved, if needed)
3 Chinese sausages (lop cheung), finely diced
4 tablespoons peanut oil, for frying

1.   To prepare the filling and the dough, follow the directions for Scallion Pancakes, *page 82*. Divide the dough into 4 equal pieces.
2.   With your hands, roll 1 piece of dough into a ball, then press down with palm. At all stages, make certain that the work surface is dusted with flour to prevent sticking. With a rolling pin, roll out the dough to a circle 9 inches in diameter.
3.   Spread 3 tablespoons of filling over the dough, then sprinkle ¼ of the diced sausage on top. Begin at one side and roll into a sausage shape, then roll into a curve, jelly-roll fashion, so that a round is created. Close the end by pressing down.

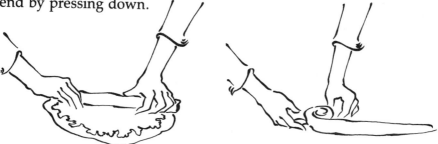

4.   Dust with flour, then roll with rolling pin to create an 8-inch round. Repeat with other 3 sections of dough.

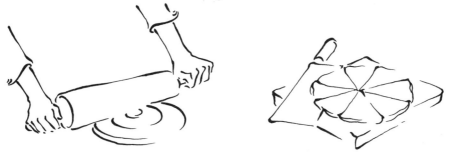

5.   Fry each pancake in the peanut oil in a cast-iron skillet over medium heat, 3 minutes on each side, or until golden brown. Drain on paper towel, place in serving dish, and cut in pie-shaped wedges to serve.

❧ Special Scallion Pancakes can be frozen for 1 or 2 months. To reheat, pan-fry or reheat in a 350°F. oven until warmed through.

GAU JI
Shanghai Dumplings or Little Dumplings
48 dumplings

In Peking these half-moon-shaped dumplings are called "chiao-tzu," which is modern Chinese for the Cantonese "gau ji." In Shanghai they are often referred to as "wor tip," two words which mean "pot" and "stick," and they are therefore known as "potstickers," a most unfortunate name in my view, for something that tastes so good. I prefer to call them by their Cantonese name, gau ji, which literally translated is "little dumplings."

Filling
      4 cups water
      1 teaspoon salt, for blanching
   1/2 teaspoon baking soda
      1 cup bok choy, white stalk, cut into 1/4-inch slices
      2 cups firmly packed bok choy leaves, torn apart, then sliced into
            1/4-inch pieces
  1 1/4 pounds ground pork
   1/2 cup finely sliced scallions
      1 egg
  1 1/2 teaspoons salt
      1 tablespoon sugar
      1 tablespoon ground ginger
      1 tablespoon white wine
      2 teaspoons light soy sauce
      1 tablespoon sesame oil
         Pinch of white pepper
      3 tablespoons cornstarch

1.   Bring the water to a boil, then add 1 teaspoon salt, the baking soda, and bok choy leaves. (The baking soda serves to make the vegetables remain bright green.) Blanch the bok choy for 1 minute, strain, then run cold tap water over the leaves. Allow the leaves to drain, then place them, half at a time, in a paper towel and squeeze out excess water.
2.   In a large bowl, combine all the remaining ingredients and add the bok choy leaves. Mix well in one direction with chopsticks or wooden spoon until thoroughly blended. Refrigerate 3 to 4 hours, or overnight.

Dough
3 cups Gold Medal flour, all-purpose, enriched, bleached
10½ ounces cold water

Place the flour in a large mixing bowl. Make a well in the center and gradually add the water. Stir with your fingers to make a firm dough. If the dough is too dry, add more water. Knead until smooth and set aside, covered with a damp cloth, for about ½ hour.

To make dumplings
1. Dust the work surface with flour. Divide the dough into 4 equal pieces. Work with 1 piece at a time, keeping the others covered with a damp cloth.
2. Roll 1 piece into a 12-inch-long sausage shape. Cut the sausage into 12 equal pieces.
3. Using a small rolling pin, roll each piece into a 3-inch round. Place the dough round in your hand. Place 1 teaspoon of filling in the middle, then close into a half-moon shape, pleating as you close it. (See directions for forming Shrimp Dumplings, *page 52*.) Repeat until all the dough and all the filling is used.
4. Pour 3 tablespoons of peanut oil into a 12-inch cast-iron skillet. Heat oil over high heat. When a wisp of smoke appears, place dumplings, 16 at a time, in skillet. Allow them to cook for 3 minutes, then pour ½ cup cold water into skillet. Cover.
5. Allow the dumplings to cook over medium heat until the water evaporates. Lower heat and continue to cook until dumplings are golden brown on the bottom and somewhat translucent on top. (To allow all dumplings to cook evenly, move the skillet back and forth over the heat so that all parts of the cooking surface receive even heat.) Remove from the skillet, place in serving dish, and serve immediately.

✄ Shanghai Dumplings may be frozen. Dust the dumplings with flour before freezing so that they do not stick together.
   To cook, allow the dumplings to return to room temperature, then proceed with steps 4 and 5.

SIU LOON BAU
Soup Dumplings
40 dumplings

The traditional method of making these dumplings was to cook fresh pig skin in water for 36 to 48 hours so that the skin dissolved in the resulting soup. When it cooled, it became gelatin. But because this takes an enormous amount of time, and the prospect of cooking pig skin for two days might not be pleasing to some, I use gelatin.

These dumplings, here made with a fresh chicken-stock base, are possibly the most famous dim sum of Shanghai, and justly so. Each dumpling, when steamed, contains a measure of liquid hot soup and the explosion of taste in one's mouth is exquisite. Very seldom do soup dumplings appear on dim sum menus because they take much time to prepare. But results of those labors are most satisfying. Many steps are involved. I recommend that you make the stock and the filling a day ahead of time, then combine them with freshly made dough for the best results. I have set the recipe down in stages, which in my opinion is the best way to proceed.

Stock
5 pounds chicken bones and skins
9 cups of water
11 cups of cold water
1 slice fresh ginger, mashed
1 clove garlic, peeled
4 scallions, ends discarded, washed and cut in half
1 medium onion, quartered
  Salt to taste
1 envelope unflavored geletin

1.   In a large pot, bring the 9 cups of water to a boil. Add chicken bones and skin and allow them to boil for 1 minute. Strain off all liquid, retaining skin and bones, then run cold tap water over them and drain.
2.   Place skin and bones in an 8-quart pot, add the 11 cups cold water, ginger, garlic, scallions, and onion. Cover and bring to a boil. Uncover and allow the stock to simmer for 5 hours. Strain contents, reserving the liquid. Discard solid ingredients. There should be about 2 cups of chicken stock. Salt the stock to suit your taste.

3.   In a saucepan, boil 1 cup of the stock. (Freeze the remaining cup of stock for future use.) Place the powdered gelatin in a mixing bowl and pour in the boiling stock. Stir, mixing well, and allow the mixture to cool to room temperature. Then refrigerate and allow the stock to harden.

Filling

     1 pound ground pork
     1/2 pound shrimp, shelled, deveined, washed, dried, and diced
     1 1/2 teaspoons salt
     1 tablespoon sugar
     2 teaspoons grated fresh ginger
     1 1/2 teaspoons sesame oil
     1 teaspoon light soy sauce
     2 teaspoons white wine
     1 egg
     3 tablespoons cornstarch
       Pinch of white pepper

In a bowl, combine all the filling ingredients. Mix in one direction until thoroughly blended. Refrigerate at least 4 hours or overnight.

Dough

     The dough for the dumpling skins can be made with either of two flours. The first, which I prefer, is Pillsbury's H & R All-Purpose Flour, which in my estimation comes closest to the traditional Chinese "noodle flour" which is nonrising and highly elastic and can thus be rolled paper thin. The second is Pillsbury's Best All-Purpose Enriched Flour, which makes fine skins, but lacks a bit of the elasticity I prefer.

1 1/4 cups flour (Pillsbury H & R preferred)
1/2 teaspoon baking soda
  2 eggs
1/4 cup Pillsbury's All-Purpose flour mixed with 1/4 cup boiling water

Mix the 1 1/4 cups of flour and the baking soda with the 2 eggs, adding 1 egg at a time as you mix. Make a well and into it pour the flour–boiling-water mixture. Begin kneading the sticky mass, dusting regularly with additional flour to prevent excessive stickiness. Knead into an elastic dough that is even in color and not streaked. When smooth, knead for

10 minutes, then set aside. Cover the dough with plastic wrap and allow it to rest for 1 hour in the summer, 4 to 5 hours in the winter.

Make dumplings

1.   Cut the gelatin into 1/4-inch dice. Mix the gelatin into the filling and set aside.
2.   Cut the dough into 4 equal pieces. Roll each section into a 10-inch-long sausage shape and cut it into 10 equal pieces. Work on 1 piece at a time; keep the remaining pieces covered with plastic wrap.
3.   Using a small rolling pin, roll each small piece into a thin 3-inch round. (To avoid sticking, sprinkle cornstarch on the work surface.) Place a round in your hand, put 1 1/2 tablespoons of filling in the center, and close the round.

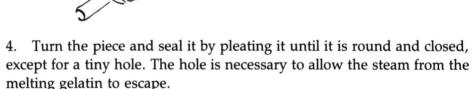

4.   Turn the piece and seal it by pleating it until it is round and closed, except for a tiny hole. The hole is necessary to allow the steam from the melting gelatin to escape.

5.   Repeat steps 3 and 4 until you have made 40 dumplings. Place the dumplings in a steamer lined with bamboo leaves, lettuce leaves, or cabbage leaves. Steam for 10 to 12 minutes. Serve hot.

✂︎ Soup dumplings cannot be frozen, and they should not be kept even overnight in the refrigerator, because the skin will crack and the soup will run out. They should be served immediately and eaten at one meal. You'll have no trouble!

DAI GUT YAU GOK
Good Luck Dumplings
36 dumplings

This is a traditional dumpling served during the New Year holiday. The results of the handwork involved, which are there for all to see, are meant to impress on a special holiday. And they do.

     2 cups Gold Medal flour
  1/4 cup sugar
     5 tablespoons lard or peanut oil
3 1/2 ounces cold water
  1/2 cup peanuts, with skins
  1/4 cup sesame seeds
3 1/2 tablespoons dark brown sugar
     4 cups peanut oil

1.   Place flour on work surface. Using your fingers, mix in the sugar. Make a well and add the lard or peanut oil. Using your fingertips, mix until the ingredients are combined. Then make another well, dribble the water in slowly, and, using the other hand, combine thoroughly. Knead the dough for 10 minutes. Set aside, covered with a damp cloth, for 2 hours.
2.   Heat wok 40 seconds over low heat. Place peanuts in the wok, spread them in a thin layer, roast for 2 minutes, turn them over, and continue roasting until they become deep brown. Remove peanuts from the wok; peel the skins and place half the peanuts on a sheet of wax paper. With a rolling pin, crush the peanuts until they are coarsely broken, but not powdery. Crush remaining peanuts in the same manner, combine with first batch, and set aside.

3.   Follow above procedure for roasting sesame seeds until brown, but do not crush them. Set aside.

4.   In a small shallow dish, combine the roasted peanuts, the sesame seeds, and the brown sugar.

5.   Cut the dough into thirds. Work with 1 section at a time, keeping the others under a damp cloth. With your hands, roll ¹/₃ of the dough into a log 12 inches long and 1 inch in diameter. With the blade of a dough scraper, cut the log into 12 1-inch pieces.

6.   Roll each piece into a ball. With a rolling pin, roll out a circle 3¹/₂ inches in diameter.

7.   Holding the piece of dough in your hand, place 1 teaspoon of filling in the center, close the edge into a half-moon shape, and pinch the seam closed, crimping to make a scalloped edge.

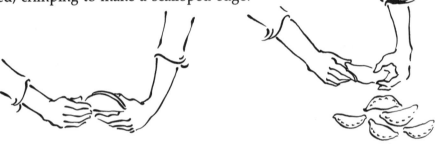

8.   In a wok, heat 4 cups of peanut oil to 325°F. Deep-fat fry the dumplings until they are golden brown. Remove, drain, and serve immediately.

✄ These dim sum can be frozen. To reheat, allow them to return to room temperature. Then, deep-fat fry lightly, or warm them in a preheated 325°F. oven. These dumplings stay crunchy even after freezing, so they are delicious simply defrosted and served at room temperature.

The Changeable Nature of Glutinous Rice

The sticky properties of glutinous rice, which allow it to be shaped into dim sum, have already been noted. But this rice has other extraordinary characteristics. In combination with such strong ingredients as Chinese sausage and Chinese bacon, it tends to borrow, and retain, their tastes and aromas, which is a lovely bonus. It makes glutinous rice very special.

Not well known to the Western palate, glutinous rice has a touch of sweetness that is almost evanescent. When touched with lotus leaves it becomes sweet with lotus. When added to congees it thickens and smooths. The Chinese almost revere glutinous rice and thus it is *always* an ingredient at holiday feasts and other special occasions.

You should note the earlier recipe for Nor Mai Guen, Glutinous Rice Loaf, which contains Chinese sausage and bacon. In addition, the recipe for Sang Chau Nor Mai Fan, Stir-Fried Glutinous Rice, which follows, when packed into little baskets fashioned from Basic Wheat Flour Dough, becomes still another dim sum called Nor Mai Siu Mai, which simply means "Glutinous Rice Siu Mai."

SANG CHAU NOR MAI FAN	*Stir-Fried Glutinous Rice*
NOR MAI SIU MAI	*Glutinous Rice Siu Mai*
NOR MAI GAI	*Stuffed Lotus Leaves*
JUN JIU KAU	*Pearl Balls*
HOM SOI GOK	*Glutinous Rice Dough Dumplings (Salt-Water Dumplings)*
JIN DUI JAI	*Glutinous Sesame Seed Dumplings*

SANG CHAU NOR MAI FAN
Stir-Fried Glutinous Rice

   2 cups glutinous rice
1/3 cup Chinese bacon, diced
1/3 cup Chinese sausage, diced
   1 tablespoon dried shrimp, soaked in hot water for 1/2 hour, then
        diced
3/4 teaspoon salt
   1 teaspoon light soy sauce
   1 teaspoon dark soy sauce
   2 tablespoons oyster sauce
   2 to 3 scallions, ends discarded, washed, dried, and finely chopped
   1 teaspoon sesame oil

1. Wash and rinse the glutinous rice 3 or 4 times and drain. In a 9-inch aluminum cake pan, place the rice and add 2 cups of fresh water. Pour 3 to 4 cups of water into a steamer, and place the steamer into a wok and bring to a boil. Place the cake pan containing the rice into the wok, cover, and steam for 25 to 35 minutes or until the rice becomes translucent.
2. Heat another wok for 30 seconds, or until hot. Put in the bacon and stir-fry it for 30 seconds, then push it to one side. Add the sausage, stir-fry for 1 minute, then combine the sausage with the bacon.
3. Add the shrimp, stir-fry for 15 seconds, then add the salt and continue stirring for another 15 seconds. Add the steamed rice, lower heat, and, using a metal spatula, continually turn the rice, mixing it with the other ingredients for about 1 minute. Add the light and the dark soy sauces, and mix thoroughly.
4. Add the oyster sauce and stir until the rice acquires an even, pale brown color and is thoroughly mixed. Add the scallions and mix well. Turn off the heat, then add the sesame oil and combine thoroughly.

5.   Pack the cooked rice into small bowls, then up-end them onto plates to create a perfect curved mound of rice. Serve immediately.

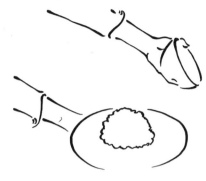

✂ Stir-Fried Glutinous Rice should not be frozen.

NOR MAI SIU MAI
Glutinous Rice Siu Mai
50 to 60 dumplings

This adaptation of traditional siu mai is my creation, a true dim sum dumpling of dough with a glutinous rice filling. The combination of the seasoned, stir-fried rice and the steamed dough skins is irresistible.

   1 recipe Stir-Fried Glutinous Rice, *page 94*
   1 recipe Basic Wheat Flour—Siu Mai Dough, *page 58* (or use won
      ton skins)

Follow directions for Siu Mai, Cook and Sell Dumplings, *page 61.*

✂These will not freeze.

NOR MAI GAI
Stuffed Lotus Leaves
8 pieces

These glutinous rice preparations are traditionally wrapped in lotus leaves, which give off a delicate and subtly sweet aroma when steamed. Unfortunately, lotus leaves are usually sold in 50-pound boxes for restaurant use, although they are becoming more readily available. If you can get lotus leaves, by all means use them, the fresher the better. If not, then bamboo leaves are equally satisfying and their aroma is equally rich. Small packages of bamboo leaves can be purchased in Chinese groceries or specialty food shops.

4 large lotus leaves or 16 large bamboo leaves, soaked in hot water for 1 or 2 hours, or until soft

For blanching
$2^{1}/_{2}$ cups cold water
$^{1}/_{4}$ teaspoon baking soda
1 scallion, washed, ends discarded, and cut in half
1 piece eight-star anise
1 2-inch piece of ginger, mashed

1 pound chicken breasts, skin and bones removed (or $^{1}/_{2}$ pound lean chicken cutlets), cut into 1-inch by 2-inch pieces
$^{1}/_{2}$ pound chicken leg, fat, skin, and membrane removed, boned, washed, dried, and cut into 1-inch pieces
$^{1}/_{4}$ pound fresh pork butt (or 1 double pork chop), cut into $^{1}/_{4}$-inch by 2-inch pieces
$^{1}/_{4}$ pound shrimp, shelled, deveined, washed, dried, and cut in half lengthwise
8 to 10 dried Chinese black mushrooms, soaked in hot water until softened, washed, excess water squeezed out, stems discarded, and caps sliced (yields about $^{1}/_{4}$ cup)

1 tablespoon peanut oil
1 tablespoon white wine

In a bowl, combine the following ingredients for a sauce:

    3 tablespoons oyster sauce
    1¼ teaspoons salt
    3¼ teaspoons sugar
    2 teaspoons dark soy sauce
    1 teaspoon light soy sauce
    2 teaspoons sesame oil
    Pinch of white pepper
    2 tablespoons cornstarch mixed with ½ cup chicken broth

1.   To blanch the chicken, chicken leg, pork, and shrimp: Place 2½ cups of cold water into the wok. Add the baking soda, the scallion, the eight-star anise, and the ginger. Bring the mixture to a boil, and let boil for 3 minutes.

2.   Add the pork, bring again to a boil, add the chicken and bring to a boil, then add the shrimp. When the shrimp turns pink and curls, remove all the ingredients from the wok and place in a strainer. Let the water drain out completely, remove the scallion, anise, and ginger, and set aside.

3.   Wash the wok and dry it thoroughly. Heat for 30 seconds over high heat. Add 1 tablespoon of peanut oil and spread it around with a metal spatula. Add the blanched ingredients and the mushrooms. Stir-fry for about 1 minute. Add the white wine, trickling it in around the edge of the wok. Mix thoroughly.

4.   Make a well in the center of the ingredients and add the sauce mixture. Mix well, quickly, until the sauce thickens and turns dark brown.

5.   Transfer mixture to a shallow dish and allow it to come to room temperature. Refrigerate covered for 2 to 3 hours, or overnight.

Preparing the glutinous rice filling

4 cups glutinous rice
2 Chinese sausages (lop cheung)
2 ounces roast pork, cut into 16 pieces

1.   In a large mixing bowl, wash the rice in cold water 3 or 4 times. Drain the rice in a strainer. Place rice in a 9-inch round cake pan. Add 4 cups cold water. Wash the 2 sausages and place them on top of the rice. Steam in a steamer for 35 to 40 minutes. Remove the sausages from the rice, and cut them into 16 equal slices. Set aside.

2.   Place the steamed rice in a large mixing bowl and add:

       3 tablespoons oyster sauce
    1$^{1}/_{2}$ teaspoons salt
    3$^{1}/_{4}$ teaspoons sugar
       2 teaspoons dark soy sauce
       1 teaspoon light soy sauce
       2 teaspoons sesame oil
         Pinch of white pepper

Mix well, preferably with hands.

Stuffing the lotus leaves
1.   Divide chicken-pork-shrimp-mushroom mixture into 8 equal portions.
2.   Prepare lotus or bamboo leaves by cutting out center stem with scissors, then cutting the leaves into 4 equal triangular parts. There will be 16 pieces.
3.   Using 2 pieces at a time, 1 overlapping the other, place $^{1}/_{2}$ cup of glutinous rice in the center. Pat it down lightly and add 1 portion of the meat mixture. Place 2 slices of roast pork and 2 pieces of Chinese sausage on top of the meat mixture. Then place another $^{1}/_{2}$ cup of rice on top of the pork and sausage.

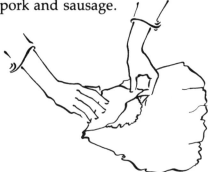

4.   Pick up the pointed end of leaves, fold inward, squeeze, then fold the broad back end over it. Roll other ends in to close the leaf. Place the stuffed leaves in a steamer and steam for $^{1}/_{2}$ hour. Remove from steamer and serve hot.

✂ Stuffed Lotus Leaves cannot be frozen. They will keep, refrigerated, for 2 to 3 days. To reheat, steam for $^{1}/_{2}$ hour.

NOTE: If you make this recipe using bamboo leaves, you will need to tie them closed, like a small package, with string.

J U N   J I U   K A U
Pearl Balls
20 pieces

This is a beautiful-looking preparation. After the pearl balls are steamed, the kernels of glutinous rice adhering to them do indeed resemble tiny seed pearls. This is not a Cantonese dim sum but one found in Shanghai, and in Peking it would be served as a first course in a banquet.

   1 cup glutinous rice
   1 pound ground pork
   4 fresh water chestnuts, peeled, washed, dried, and cut into ⅛-inch
      dice
   2 scallions, ends discarded, washed, dried, and finely sliced
1½ teaspoons minced fresh ginger
   1 large egg, beaten
1½ tablespoons cornstarch mixed with 2 tablespoons cold water
1¼ teaspoons salt
2½ teaspoons sugar
   1 teaspoon sesame oil
   2 teaspoons light soy sauce
1½ teaspoons white wine
     Pinch of white pepper
   2 tablespoons peanut oil

1.   Wash the rice, and, in a bowl, soak it for 1 hour. Drain. In a strainer, dry the rice for 2 hours.

2.   In a bowl, combine all ingredients except rice. Mix in one direction with wooden spoon or 2 pairs of chopsticks until it becomes soft, thoroughly mixed, and all ingredients stick together.

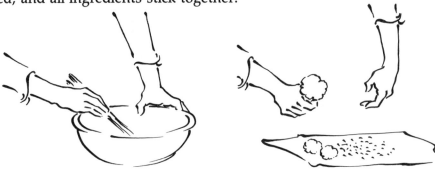

3.   Pick up a handful of the mixture, move it around in the hand gently, then squeeze. The amount that oozes through the top of the hand will be a ball about 1 inch in diameter. Repeat for rest of mixture.

4.   Place all the balls (about 20) on a sheet of wax paper. On a second sheet of wax paper, smooth the rice into a thin layer.

5.   Roll each pork ball through the rice so that it receives a single coating of kernels.

6.   Line steamer with green lettuce leaves. Place pearl balls on lettuce and steam for about 15 to 20 minutes, or until rice becomes translucent and pork cooks through. Serve immediately.

✄ These cannot be frozen.

HOM SOI GOK
Glutinous Rice Dough Dumplings (Salt-Water Dumplings)
48 dumplings

This dim sum, and the one that follows, are made with a special flour, really a powder made from ground glutinous rice. Though they are deep-fried, they tend not to be crisp, but rather chewy and elastic. It is this softer, shifting consistency, and the fact that hom soi gok are salty, that led the Cantonese to call these New Year specialties "salt-water dumplings."

Dough

2 cups glutinous rice powder mixed with 7 ounces of cold water
3/4 cup wheat starch mixed with 7 ounces boiling water
1/2 teaspoon salt
4 tablespoons lard

In a very large mixing bowl, combine all the ingredients and mix thoroughly. Place the dough on a floured work surface and knead for 15 minutes. Cover dough with plastic wrap and refrigerate for 3 hours.

Filling

1/2 pound fresh pork, coarsely ground
1/4 pound shrimp, shelled, deveined, washed, dried, diced into
     1/8-inch pieces

Marinade for pork and shrimp

1 teaspoon salt
2 1/2 teaspoons sugar
1 teaspoon sesame oil
2 teaspoons light soy sauce
1 1/2 tablespoons oyster sauce
Pinch of white pepper

1 1/2 tablespoons peanut oil
1/2 cup bamboo shoots, diced
1/3 cup Chinese dried black mushrooms, soaked, washed, squeezed
     free of water, stems discarded, and caps diced in 1/8-inch
     pieces
1 tablespoon white wine
4 teaspoons cornstarch and 4 tablespoons chicken broth combined
     in a small bowl

1.   Marinate pork and shrimp for 1 hour.
2.   Heat the oil in a wok at high heat. When a wisp of white smoke appears, add the pork and the shrimp. Stir-fry for 2 to 3 minutes.
3.   Add the bamboo shoots and the mushrooms and stir well. Add the white wine, and mix thoroughly. Make a well in the center of the ingredients and pour in the cornstarch mixture. With a metal spatula, scoop ingredients over the well and mix thoroughly until the sauce thickens. Remove the

filling from the wok and place it in a shallow dish. Cool it to room temperature, then refrigerate it for 2 to 3 hours.

To make the dumplings

1.   Remove the dough from the refrigerator and knead it for 1 minute. Roll it into a log 8 inches long and 2½ inches in diameter. Divide the log into 4 equal pieces. Work with 1 piece at a time, and keep the others covered with plastic wrap.

2.   Roll each piece into a 14-inch-long sausage. Cut the sausage into 14 equal parts, each about 1 inch long. Again, work with 1 piece at a time, keeping the others covered with plastic wrap.

3.   Take a 1-inch piece, squeeze it, and roll it into a ball. Place it on a lightly floured surface and flatten it with your palm. With the blade of a lightly oiled cleaver, press down on the piece of dough, forming a circle of dough about 3 inches in diameter.

4.   Place 1½ teaspoons of filling in the center of the dough circle. Use your thumb to smooth the filling. Fold the dough around the filling, forming a half-moon. Pinch the edges tightly to seal. Place the dumpling on a platter and cover with plastic wrap. Repeat steps 3 and 4 with remaining dough to form 48 dumplings.

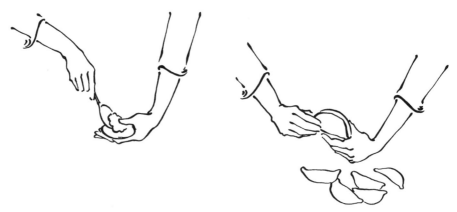

5.   In 4 to 5 cups of peanut oil heated to 325° to 350°F., deep-fat fry the dumplings for 2 to 3 minutes until light brown. Drain and serve immediately.

✄ These can be frozen. To reheat: Allow dumplings to return to room temperature, then deep-fat fry for 2 to 3 minutes.

JIN DUI JAI
Glutinous Sesame Seed Dumplings
30 to 35 dumplings

These dim sum are favored by Buddhist monks during the New Year celebrations. A truly observant Buddhist, for example, attaches so much importance to this preparation that he would not prepare it unless the day was propitious, according to the Chinese calendar. But you can make it anytime, whether or not you are a Buddhist or a monk.

1/2 recipe (2 cups) Red Bean Paste Filling, *page 76*, or 1 can of commercial red bean paste
 1 recipe Glutinous Rice Dough, *page 101*
1/3 cup white sesame seeds
 4 to 5 cups peanut oil

1.   Prepare the filling and the dough.
2.   Follow steps 4 through 6 for preparing Glutinous Rice Dough Dumplings, *page 100*.
3.   Place 1 1/2 teaspoons of filling in the center of the dough circle. Gather up the sides of the dough, and, with your fingers, turn and crimp until the dough is formed into a round shape. Roll the dumpling in white sesame seeds and pat it lightly to make sure the seeds adhere.

4.   In 4 or 5 cups of peanut oil, deep-fat fry for 7 to 9 minutes until dumplings are golden brown. Drain and serve.

✄ These can be frozen. To reheat: Allow dumplings to return to room temperature and deep-fat fry for 2 to 3 minutes.

粥 Congees

The Cantonese call it "jook," a flat little word meaning "soft rice," but the name is one revered by infant and great-grandmother alike, and by all generations in between.

Mythology has it that once a rich but miserly man, faced with the need to produce sufficient rice for 10 guests, kept telling his cook to add ladles of water to the pot to stretch the rice. What resulted, the Chinese say, was a frustrated cook with a rice porridge, rather than rice. Today's congees are quite a bit more sophisticated than that and definitely *not* for the miserly.

Congee, a thickened rice soup of almost a porridge consistency, is the basis for morning breakfast in virtually all Cantonese and Shanghai households. It is what babies are raised on, and it is often the centerpiece of such significant family gatherings as weddings or sixtieth-birthday celebrations—but it is equally important as one part of the dim sum breakfast. Its variations are infinite. It is for meat eaters, fish lovers, and vegetarians. It is, in short, a perfect wonder of a thick soup.

JOOK	*Basic Congee*
PEI DAN SAU YOOK JOOK	*Preserved Egg and Pork Congee*
YUEH JOOK	*Fish Congee*
NGAU YOOK JOOK	*Beef Congee*
SANG CHOY JOOK	*Lettuce Congee*
BOK CHOY JOOK	*Bok Choy Congee*

104

JOOK
Basic Congee
6 to 8 servings

This is my basic congee recipe, and it can be eaten as is. Cantonese people often add sugar or rock candy to sweeten it, while people from Shanghai often prefer to add hot pickled cabbage to their congee.

On the following pages, I have included 5 of my favorite variations on the basic congee recipe. All are very different—all are delicious!

1/2 cup rice (I prefer short-grain rice for this, rather than the long
　　　grain. It blends better with the glutinous rice.)
1/4 cup glutinous rice
41/2 cups water
　4 cups chicken broth (*see note*)

1.　In a 4-quart pot, place both kinds of rice. Wash the rice 3 times in cold water. Drain.
2.　Return the washed rice to the pot, then add the water and the chicken broth and bring to a boil. Cover the pot, leaving the lid partially ajar. Reduce the heat to low-medium, and cook for 1 to 1 1/2 hours, stirring occasionally to prevent the rice from sticking to the bottom. Cook until the rice thickens almost to the consistency of porridge.
3.　Warm your serving tureen or bowl by "washing" it with boiling water. Add the congee to the tureen. Serve immediately.

NOTE: If you are a vegetarian, you can substitute vegetable stock for the chicken broth in this recipe.

皮
蛋
瘦
肉
粥

PEI DAN SAU YOOK JOOK
Preserved Egg and Pork Congee
6 to 8 servings

  1 Basic Congee recipe, *page 105*
  4 cups cold water, for water-blanching
 1/2 teaspoon baking soda
1 1/2 pounds lean pork butt, or fresh ham, cut into 2 pieces
  2 teaspoons sesame oil
  2 teaspoons light soy sauce
 1/2 teaspoon salt
1 1/2 teaspoons sugar
    Pinch of white pepper
  2 preserved eggs (*see note*)

1.　Prepare the Basic Congee. As the congee is cooking, prepare the pork and the egg.

2.　Water-blanch the pork: Place water in wok, add baking soda, bring to a boil. Place the pork pieces into the water and boil for 2 minutes. Turn off the heat and pour the water out of the wok. Place the pork in a bowl filled with cold water and allow it to rest for 15 minutes.

3.　Remove the pork from the cold water. Cut it into 1/2-inch-thick slices. With the side of a cleaver, pound the slices to break the fibers. Cut the slices into long 1/2-inch slivers, then dice.

4.　In a bowl, place the sesame oil, the light soy sauce, the salt, the sugar, and the white pepper. Add the diced pork, mix well, and set aside.

5.　Remove the coatings and shells from the preserved eggs. Wash and dry. Chop the eggs into small pieces and set aside.

6.　About 20 minutes before the congee is finished cooking, add the pork and the preserved egg to the cooking rice. Mix thoroughly, and allow to simmer until the pork is thoroughly cooked. Transfer to a tureen and serve immediately.

NOTE: Preserved eggs are often called thousand-year-old eggs, and they often look as if they had been coated with charcoal or with clay and husks of grain. They are available in Chinese grocery stores and in some specialty food shops.

YUEH JOOK
Fish Congee
6 to 8 servings

1 Basic Congee recipe, *page 105*
1 3-pound fresh fish (1 3-pound fish—carp, sea bass, sole, or floun-
    der—yields 1½ pounds when prepared)

Combine in a small bowl to make a marinade:
    1 teaspoon white vinegar
    2 tablespoons white wine
    2 teaspoons light soy sauce
    2 teaspoons sesame oil
    2 tablespoons peanut oil
    1 teaspoon salt
      Pinch of white pepper
    4 to 6 slices of ginger, peeled and julienned
    2 scallions, ends discarded, washed, dried, and cut into
        1½-inch sections
    1 tablespoon Scallion Oil, *page 166*
    ⅛ teaspoon white pepper
    1 teaspoon light soy sauce
    3 scallions, finely sliced for garnish
    1 tablespoon chopped coriander (optional)

1.   Prepare the Basic Congee. As the congee is cooking, prepare the fish.
2.   Place the fish in a heatproof dish. Make sure the marinade is mixed
well, then pour it over the fish. Place pieces of ginger and scallions
beneath the fish, in the body cavity, and on top of it. Steam the fish for
15 minutes.
3.   Remove the fish from the steamer and allow it to cool to room temperature. Discard the skin, bones, ginger, and scallions, and break fish
flesh into very small pieces.
4.   In a bowl, place the fish pieces. Add the scallion oil, white pepper,
and light soy sauce. Mix lightly with chopsticks. When the Basic Congee
is done, add the fish to it. Mix together and allow the congee to come
to a boil.
5.   Pour the congee into the serving tureen and top with sliced scallions

or coriander. Present the congee, but before serving, stir the scallions into the soup.

NGAU YOOK JOOK
Beef Congee
6 to 8 servings

    1 Basic Congee recipe, *page 105*
    1 pound ground beef
    4 fresh water chestnuts, peeled, washed, dried, and diced
    3 scallions, ends discarded, washed, dried, and sliced fine
    2 teaspoons fresh peeled ginger, minced
    1 egg, beaten
 1½ tablespoons cornstarch mixed with 2 tablespoons cold water
 1¼ teaspoons salt
 2½ teaspoons sugar
 1½ teaspoons sesame oil
 1½ teaspoons light soy sauce
    1 teaspoon blended whiskey
    2 tablespoons peanut oil
      Pinch of white pepper
      Finely sliced scallions for garnish

1. Cook Basic Congee and, when done, turn off heat and set aside.
2. In the bowl of an electric mixer, combine all the remaining ingredients. Mix at low speed for 3 minutes, then at medium speed for 3 to 4 minutes, or until all ingredients are thoroughly blended.
3. Turn the heat on low under the congee. Using a teaspoon, scoop up a small ball of the beef mixture and push it gently off the spoon with your finger into the congee. Repeat until all the beef is used.
4. Slowly bring the congee to a boil. When it boils, the beef is done.
5. Garnish the congee with finely sliced scallions and serve immediately.

S A N G   C H O Y   J O O K
Lettuce Congee
6 to 8 servings

   1 Basic Congee recipe, *page 105*
   8 cups of lettuce (*see note*)
1½ to 2 teaspoons salt
   2 teaspoons light soy sauce
     Pinch of white pepper
   1 slice of fresh ginger
   2 to 3 tablespoons of Scallion Oil, *page 166*

1.   Prepare the Basic Congee. As the congee is cooking, wash the lettuce thoroughly and cut into ⅓-inch by 4-inch pieces.
2.   When the congee is done, add the lettuce, salt, soy sauce, white pepper, and ginger. Mix thoroughly, then bring the congee to a boil, stirring constantly. Add the Scallion Oil and mix well. Serve hot.

NOTE: Use any kind of lettuce you like. I prefer iceberg but you can also use romaine, Boston, or Bibb lettuce.

B O K   C H O Y   J O O K
Bok Choy Congee
6 to 8 servings

   1 Basic Congee recipe, *page 105*
   3 cups white stalks of bok choy
   5 cups bok choy leaves
1½ to 2 teaspoons salt
   2 teaspoons light soy sauce
     Pinch of white pepper
   1 slice of fresh ginger
   2 to 3 tablespoons Scallion Oil, *page 166*

1.   Prepare the Basic Congee. As the congee is cooking, wash the bok choy stalks and leaves. Cut the leaves into ¼-inch by 4-inch slices, and the stalks into ¼-inch pieces.

2.   About 10 to 15 minutes before the congee is completely cooked, add the bok choy stalks, salt, soy sauce, pepper, and ginger. Mix together thoroughly and bring the congee to a boil, stirring constantly. Reduce the heat. Add the Scallion Oil and mix well. Add the bok choy leaves and cook for 2 or 3 minutes. Serve hot.

蝦 The Ubiquitous Shrimp

By this point you will have noted the extensive use of shrimp in dim sum. This is no accident. To the Cantonese, the word for shrimp is "har," which is also the word which is the sound of laughter. Shrimp is regarded as a most felicitous food and is used in an uncountable number of ways as a main ingredient, as an accompaniment, and often as a subtle flavoring. No banquet, perhaps no Cantonese meal, is regarded as whole until the shrimp appears in some form to be eaten.

This section is devoted to shrimp as a prime filling for dim sum. Using the basic Cantonese filling, truly a classic recipe, you will be able to illustrate the compatibility of shrimp with other foods. Also included is that favorite dim sum of many people, shrimp toast.

HAR HOM	*Basic Shrimp Filling*
YUNG HAI KIM	*Stuffed Crab Claws*
HAH YUEN	*Round Shrimp*
YUNG DAU FU	*Stuffed Bean Curd*
BOK FAR SIU MAI	*Stuffed Mushrooms*
LAH CHIU	*Pepper Siu Mai*
HAR DOR SEE	*Shrimp Toast*

HAR HOM
Basic Shrimp Filling

This is a classic Cantonese filling used in various dim sum. When thoroughly blended and allowed to stand, refrigerated, for about 4 hours, it acquires an elegant and delicate taste that complements many other foods perfectly. It can be served as an hors d'oeuvre or used as a first course for a meal that may, in fact, not even be Chinese.

      2 pounds shrimp, shelled, deveined, washed, dried, and quartered
           (yielding about 1¾ pounds)
1¾ teaspoons salt
2½ teaspoons sugar
   ½ cup winter bamboo shoots, cut into ⅛-inch dice
      4 scallions, ends discarded, washed, dried, and finely sliced
1½ egg whites, beaten
      2 teaspoons oyster sauce
      2 teaspoons sesame oil
      2 teaspoons white wine
   ⅛ teaspoon white pepper

1.   In the bowl of an electric mixer, place shrimp and salt, and mix for 2 minutes at low speed. Add sugar; mix for another 2 minutes. Add bamboo shoots, scallions, and egg whites and mix for 2 more minutes. Add remaining ingredients and mix for 5 minutes.

2.   Place the mixture in a shallow bowl and refrigerate for at least 4 hours. (It is much easier to stuff the dim sum when the mixture is cold.) When thoroughly chilled, use it to fill the various dim sum in the 5 following recipes.

✂ Basic Shrimp Filling can be frozen, and will keep in a covered dish for 1 to 2 weeks.

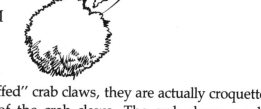

YUNG HAI KIM
Stuffed Crab Claws
12 to 14 claws

Although these are called "stuffed" crab claws, they are actually croquettes molded around the outside of the crab claws. The crab claws can be purchased at any fish market.

  1 Basic Shrimp Filling recipe, *page 112*
12–14 crab (medium hard-shelled) claws
  4 tablespoons plus ¾ cup tapioca flour for dusting
  5 cups peanut oil

1.   Prepare Basic Shrimp Filling and make sure it is completely chilled.
2.   Steam the crab claws for 10 to 12 minutes and set aside.
3.   Sprinkle the surfaces of 2 cookie sheets or baking pans with the 4 tablespoons of tapioca flour, covering completely. In a shallow dish, place ¾ cup of tapioca flour.
4.   Take a handful of the filling and, with an opening-closing motion of the hand, smooth the filling into a ball. Then make a fist and remove excess filling as it comes through hand on the thumb side. Each ball should be about 2 inches in diameter. Place the balls on a floured cookie sheet or pan.

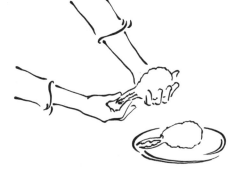

5.   Press a crab claw, meat side down, into the center of each ball of filling. Coat hands with tapioca flour from bowl; lift crab claw and filling from the sheet with both hands. Pack filling gently around claw, dusting with tapioca flour as you do so. Gently pack filling against claw with one hand, turning it with the other. Seal the filling around the claw with the pinky finger. Continue this until a smooth, croquette-shaped covering

is achieved. Place the claws on another cookie sheet or pan. Repeat until all claws are coated.

6.   Heat peanut oil in wok to 350° to 375°F. Place 2 to 3 crab claws in the oil at a time and fry until golden brown. Drain and serve immediately.

✂ The crab claws can be frozen after frying. To reheat, either fry lightly in peanut oil or warm them in a preheated 350°F. oven until they are hot.

H A H   Y U E N
Round Shrimp
About 15 pieces

½ Basic Shrimp Filling recipe, *page 112*
   4 tablespoons tapioca flour, plus ¾ cup of tapioca flour in a separate shallow bowl
   4–5 cups peanut oil, for frying

1.   Dust a cookie sheet or a baking pan with the 4 tablespoons tapioca flour so that the entire surface is covered.
2.   Take a handful of filling and press gently into a ball, discarding that which passes out of hand at thumb opening.

3.   Form a ball about 2 inches in diameter and place shrimp balls on the floured surface of the sheet or pan.
4.   Dust your hands with the tapioca flour in the bowl and, with both hands, pick up a ball of filling. Gently form into a perfect ball, coating with tapioca flour as you do so. Toss the ball from hand to hand gently,

allowing it to fall into the palm of each hand. This makes the ball firm. Place each ball, as it is finished, back on the floured cookie sheet.

5.   Heat oil to 325° to 350°F. Before placing each ball in oil, firm it up again. Deep-fat fry, 2 or 3 at a time, until golden brown, drain, and serve.

✂— These may not be frozen, but can be prepared a day ahead of time and stored, covered, in the refrigerator. To reheat, deep-fat fry for 3 to 4 minutes.

Y U N G   D A U   F U
Stuffed Bean Curd
16 pieces

For this dish I would prefer that you use Chinese bean curd rather than Japanese or Korean. Bean curd should always be purchased *fresh,* and stored in a container of fresh water in the refrigerator. Bean curd will stay fresh for 2 to 3 weeks if the water is changed daily.

¼ Basic Shrimp Filling recipe, *page 112*
  8 cakes fresh bean curd
    Tapioca flour for dusting
  3–4 tablespoons peanut oil

1.   Remove bean curd from water, place in a strainer over a bowl, and allow to drain 3 or 4 hours. Pat dry with a paper towel.

2.   Cut each cake diagonally and, with a pointed knife, cut out a pocket in each half of the curd.

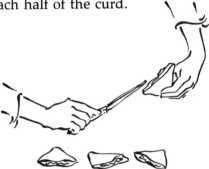

3.   Dust the pocket with tapioca flour, then fill with 1 tablespoon of the Shrimp Filling. Pack smoothly with a knife or with your fingers.

Stuffed Bean Curd may be cooked in any of the following 3 ways:
Steam for 8 to 10 minutes, until shrimp turns pink in color. Serve immediately.

or

In a cast-iron frying pan, pour 2 to 3 tablespoons of peanut oil. Heat over high heat until a wisp of white smoke appears. With the stuffed side of the bean curd down, pan-fry over medium heat for 6 minutes. Turn the cakes and cook each side for 2 minutes. Serve hot.

or

Deep-fat fry, 2 to 3 at a time, in peanut oil heated to 325°F. for about 8 minutes, or until the bean curd is golden brown. Drain and serve.

✂ Stuffed Bean Curd cannot be frozen, but it can be prepared a day ahead of time and refrigerated until ready to cook.

BOK FAR SIU MAI
Stuffed Mushrooms
24 pieces

½ Basic Shrimp Filling recipe, *page 112*
24 silver-dollar-sized Chinese dried black mushrooms

 ½ teaspoon salt
 1 teaspoon sugar
 ½ teaspoon dark soy sauce
 2 scallions, ends discarded, washed, dried, and cut into 2-inch slices
 1 ounce raw chicken fat, cut into 2 pieces
 1 slice fresh ginger, smashed with cleaver blade
   Tapioca flour

1.   Soak the mushrooms in hot water for 1 hour. Wash thoroughly and squeeze out the excess water. Remove the stems and place the mushrooms in a heat-proof dish.
2.   Add the salt, sugar, and soy sauce to the dish and toss with mushrooms.
3.   On top of the mushrooms, place the scallions, chicken fat, and ginger. In a steamer, steam them for ½ hour. Set aside.
4.   In the cavity of each mushroom, sprinkle tapioca to bind the filling to the mushroom. Pack each mushroom with 1 to 1½ tablespoons of Basic Shrimp Filling. With your finger, smooth the filling and gently press it down to make sure it won't fall out.

5.   These mushrooms can be steamed or pan-fried: Steam them for 4 to 6 minutes or until shrimp turns pink; or pan-fry them until the mushrooms and the filling brown. If you pan-fry the mushrooms, drain them before serving.

✄—These cannot be frozen, but they can be prepared and stuffed a day in advance and stored, covered, in the refrigerator. To reheat, pan-fry for 3 to 4 minutes.

118

LAH CHIU
Pepper Siu Mai
About 20 pieces

2 medium red bell peppers
2 medium green bell peppers
 Tapioca flour for dusting
½ Basic Shrimp Filling recipe, *page 112*

1. Wash, dry, and seed the peppers. Cut into lengthwise quarters and remove membranes. Slice each quarter lengthwise, making 8 pieces.
2. Sprinkle a bit of tapioca flour into the cavity of each piece of pepper, then pack 1 to 1½ tablespoons of shrimp filling into it with a knife or with your fingers.

3. Stuffed peppers can be either steamed or pan-fried. Steam for 5 to 7 minutes, or pan-fry until golden brown. If you use the pan-fry method, drain the peppers before serving.

✄ These cannot be frozen, but can be prepared and stuffed a day ahead and stored, covered, in the refrigerator. To reheat, place in a steamer for 3 to 4 minutes or until the peppers are warmed through.

HAR DOR SEE
Shrimp Toast
32 dumplings

Cantonese chefs created this dim sum with a slightly Western touch. The use of bread, not a traditionally common foodstuff in southern China, makes them unique, and thus, as you might expect, shrimp toast is a great favorite of both non-Chinese people and Chinese people alike.

½ pound raw shrimp, shelled, deveined, washed, dried thoroughly, and chopped fine
¼ pound pork fat, cut into very fine dice
½ pound onions, cut into very fine dice (*see note*)

In a small dish combine:
1 teaspoon ginger juice (*see note*)
1 teaspoon white wine

1½ teaspoons salt
1¼ teaspoons sugar
1 teaspoon sesame oil
2 teaspoons oyster sauce
Pinch of white pepper
1 egg
3½ tablespoons cornstarch
18 slices good white bread (*see note*)
1 egg, beaten
4 to 5 cups peanut oil for deep-fat frying

1.　In a bowl, combine the shrimp, pork fat, onions, and the ginger juice mixed with white wine from the small dish. Immediately add salt, sugar, sesame oil, oyster sauce, white pepper, egg, and cornstarch. With chopsticks or wooden spoon, stir in one direction until the mixture is thoroughly combined. Refrigerate for 2 to 3 hours or until the mixture is completely chilled.

2.　Trim the crusts from 8 slices of the bread, then cut each of these slices diagonally to form triangles. Reserve the crust.

To make bread crumbs

Preheat oven to 325°F. On a cookie sheet or baking pan, place the remaining 10 slices of bread and the reserved crusts from the slices used in step 2. Bake the bread for 15 to 20 minutes, or until it is hard and golden brown. Put this toast, a few pieces at a time, into a blender or food processor and blend until the crumbs are fine (yields about 2 cups).

1.   Mound 1 tablespoon of the chilled filling onto a bread triangle. Using your fingers, seal the shrimp mixture with the beaten egg. Cover the shrimp mixture evenly with the bread crumbs and, with your fingers, pat and shape into a pyramidlike mound. Shake off any excess bread crumbs.

2.   Deep-fat fry at 325° to 350°F. for 5 to 7 minutes or until golden brown. Serve immediately.

NOTE: Try to use older onions as opposed to fresh ones. Younger onions contain a great deal of water and tend to make the shrimp toasts too soggy.

I recommend Pepperidge Farm White Bread or Arnold's Brick Oven White Bread. Allow the bread to stand for about 15 minutes, so that it begins to dry out.

To make ginger juice

Peel a small piece of fresh ginger. Grate ginger with a hand grater, then squeeze the grated ginger through a garlic press. Although ginger juice can be bought ready-made, I do not recommend it, because it is too diluted for my taste and the flavor it imparts is weak.

❧Shrimp Toasts cannot be frozen, but, after cooking, they can be refrigerated for 2 or 3 days. To reheat, either warm them in a 350°F. oven or deep-fat fry. The latter is preferred.

Spring Rolls: A Seasonal Greeting

Spring rolls, in their many forms, are favorites in southeastern China from Canton to Shanghai. The Cantonese for spring roll is "chun guen," and it is quite literally a celebration of that season. Spring begins for the Chinese on New Year's Day, the first day of the lunar calendar, and spring rolls are one of the traditional foods served as a New Year's Day observance. Gastronomically the season is celebrated by the spring roll filled with scallions—often called spring onions—and with tender young bamboo shoots and the crispness of fresh water chestnuts.

Spring rolls are small and delicate when made correctly and much favored as a dim sum. Often they are called egg rolls, which is a Western misnomer. There are egg rolls in China but they are not those log-size, thick-skinned items we so often see in restaurants. Rather they are spring-roll size, with skins just a bit thicker, and with shredded egg pancakes added to the filling.

CHUN GUEN PEI   *Spring Roll Skins*
KWANGTUNG CHUN GUEN   *Cantonese Spring Rolls*
HOI SIN CHUN GUEN   *Imperial Seafood Rolls*
SUN TAK CHUN GUEN   *Sun Tak Spring Rolls*
SHANGHAI CHUN GUEN   *Shanghai Spring Rolls*

121

CHUN GUEN PEI
Spring Roll Skins
40 to 50 skins

Spring roll skins can be bought packaged—in either round or square shapes—in Chinese groceries and occasionally in grocery stores or supermarkets. The so-called "Shanghai" spring roll skins, which are whiter and thinner, are preferable to the thicker, darker-colored, yellowish skins. The thin skins come in 4-ounce packages of 10 skins; the thicker skins come in 1- or 2-pound packages. Both are often labeled "egg roll skins," which is a misnomer.

I would prefer that you buy the skins because making them from scratch is a good deal of work. Nevertheless, if you do not have access to a Chinese grocery and if your market does not stock ready-made spring roll skins, or if you wish to have the satisfaction of making something that is truly an achievement, then make your own from scratch.

4½ cups Pillsbury's Bleached flour
1½ teaspoons salt
2¼ cups cold water

1.   In a large mixing bowl, combine the flour and the salt. Slowly add the water, using your fingers to mix the ingredients until they are well combined. Knead the dough by hand for about 20 minutes or until it has an elastic texture. Cover the dough with a damp cloth and let rest at room temperature for 3 to 4 hours. You can store the dough in the refrigerator overnight, but you must allow it to return to room temperature before you begin to make the skins.
2.   Wash and dry a griddle. Make sure it is free of excess grease.
3.   Place the griddle over low heat. Grasp a large handful of dough from the bowl, hold it up and rotate your wrist in a constant slow motion. Keep the dough held upward, working it with fingers and palm.

4.   Quickly press the dough onto the center of the griddle using a circular motion, reverse the motion once, then quickly pull back, leaving a thin layer of dough on the griddle.

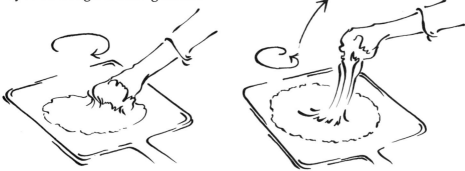

5.   The dough will start to dry on the edges in about 10 to 12 seconds. Peel the skin from the griddle and put it on a large plate. After you have made 5 or 6 skins, wrap them in a damp cloth to prevent their drying out.

❧Skins must be prepared at least a day in advance of cooking. To store, wrap them in a damp cloth, place the cloth-wrapped skins in a plastic bag, and refrigerate. Spring Roll Skins can be stored for up to 4 days or can be frozen for 1 to 2 months.

KWANGTUNG CHUN GUEN
Cantonese Spring Rolls
30 rolls

30 or more Spring Roll Skins, *page 122* (or use packaged skins)
 3 cups peanut oil, for oil-blanching
1/4 pound fresh pork, or the meat from 1 large center-cut pork chop,
    shredded
1/4 pound shrimp, washed, shelled, deveined, and quartered
 5 fresh water chestnuts, peeled, washed, dried, thinly sliced, and
    shredded
1 3/4 cups bamboo shoots, shredded
 6 to 8 scallions, ends discarded, washed, dried, cut into 1 1/2-inch
    pieces, then shredded
 1 tablespoon white wine

Combine in a small bowl:
    2 1/2 tablespoons cornstarch
     3/4 teaspoon salt
    1 1/2 teaspoons sugar
     2 teaspoons dark soy sauce
     2 tablespoons oyster sauce
      Pinch of white pepper
     1/2 cup chicken broth

1 1/2 teaspoons sesame oil
 1 egg, beaten

1.   Heat a wok for 40 seconds, add the peanut oil, and heat to 325°F.
To blanch: Place the shredded pork in the oil, gently separating the
shreds. Add the shrimp, also separating the pieces. Add water chestnuts,
bamboo shoots, and scallions, and allow the ingredients to blanch for 1
to 2 minutes. Remove the contents with a strainer and drain over a large
bowl until most of the oil has dripped through. Mix occasionally with
chopsticks.
2.   Pour the oil into a heatproof bowl, and wash the wok. Dry it and
heat for 40 seconds. Put in the ingredients from the strainer. Over very
high heat, stir-fry for 1 to 2 minutes, then add the white wine around
the edge of the wok. Mix thoroughly.

3.   Make a well in the center of the ingredients, pour in the sauce from the small bowl, and mix together quickly, using a metal spatula. Stir-fry until the sauce thickens and becomes dark. Turn off the heat, add the sesame oil, and mix well.

4.   Place the filling in a shallow dish and allow it to cool to room temperature. Refrigerate, covered, for 4 hours, or overnight.

5.   To make the spring rolls: Spread out skins. One 6-inch skin will make a cocktail-size spring roll. If you want to make larger spring rolls, use 2 skins, overlapping one with the other.

6.   Place 1 to 1½ tablespoons of the filling in a thin line at one end of the skin. Dip your fingers into the beaten egg, rub the egg along the edge of the skin, and begin folding. Keep rubbing the beaten egg along the edges as you continue folding to ensure that the spring roll will be sealed. Press and seal the end closed.

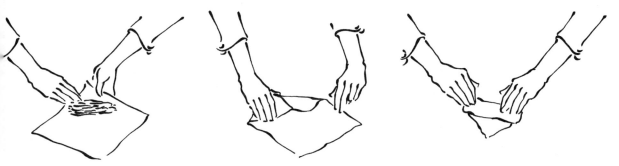

7.   Deep-fat fry 2 or 3 at a time at 325° to 350°F., until golden brown. Drain and serve.

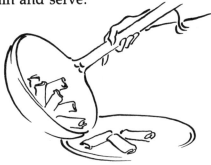

✺ Cantonese Spring Rolls can be frozen after cooking. To reheat, either deep-fat fry lightly (at 325°F.) or heat in a preheated 375°F. oven until hot.

HOI SIN CHUN GUEN

Imperial Seafood Rolls

15 rolls

15 or more Spring Roll Skins, *page 122* (or use packaged skins)
 3 tablespoons peanut oil
½ pound shrimp, washed, shelled, deveined, dried thoroughly, and
    shredded
 4 teaspoons white wine
 1 cup crabmeat
 8 to 10 scallions, ends discarded, washed, dried, cut into 1½-inch
    pieces, then shredded
 4 water chestnuts, peeled, washed, sliced fine
 4 Chinese dried mushrooms, soaked in water, dried, and shredded

Combine in a bowl:
    2 teaspoons oyster sauce
    1 teaspoon light soy sauce
    1 teaspoon sesame oil
    1 teaspoon salt
    1 teaspoon sugar
    4 teaspoons cornstarch
      Pinch of white pepper
    4 to 5 teaspoons chicken broth

 1 egg, beaten
     or
 2 tablespoons cornstarch, mixed with 2 tablespoons cold water, and 6
    ounces boiling water

1.   Heat 1½ tablespoons of the peanut oil in a wok over very high heat. When a wisp of white smoke appears, add shrimp and stir. Add the white wine by dribbling it in around the edge of the wok. Add crabmeat. Mix together thoroughly and set aside in a small dish.

2.   Wash wok. Heat over high heat for 40 seconds. Add the remaining 1½ tablespoons of peanut oil. Add the scallions, stir-fry 10 seconds; add the water chestnuts and stir-fry another 10 seconds; add the mushrooms and again stir-fry for 10 seconds. Mix thoroughly.

3.   Add shrimp and crabmeat mixture, and mix well. Create a well, add the sauce, reduce the heat, and mix until the sauce thickens and becomes dark.

4.   Remove the filling from the wok, place in a shallow dish, and allow to cool to room temperature. Refrigerate for at least 4 hours, or overnight.
5.   To make the seafood rolls: Follow steps 5, 6, and 7 of the Cantonese Spring Rolls recipe, *page 124*. Seal either with the beaten egg rubbed along edges or with a paste made by combining the 2 tablespoons cornstarch with the cold water, then adding the boiling water and smoothing the mixture into a paste.

✂ Imperial Seafood Rolls can be frozen. To reuse, either deep-fat fry lightly at 325°F. or heat through in a preheated 375°F. oven.

SUN TAK CHUN GUEN
Sun Tak Spring Rolls
15 to 20 rolls

Sun Tak, a region just outside of Canton, is the place where I was born. Our spring rolls are simpler in content than the Imperial Seafood Rolls, but equally delicious, I think. Notice that our cooking technique is quite different too.

15 to 20 Spring Roll Skins, *page 122* (or use packaged skins)
  6 ounces raw shrimp, washed, shelled, deveined, dried thoroughly, shredded, and marinated for ½ hour in:

  ½ teaspoon salt
  ¼ teaspoon light soy sauce

¼ pound fresh pork, uncooked, shredded, and marinated for ½ hour in:

  ½ teaspoon salt
  ¼ teaspoon light soy sauce

  1 bunch scallions, ends discarded, washed, dried, cut into 1½-inch pieces, and shredded
1½ tablespoons peanut oil
  1 pound bean sprouts, washed, drained, and patted dry

1. Place marinated shrimp in small bowl, ready for preparation, and do likewise with marinated pork.
2. Place scallions alongside, ready for preparation.
3. Heat wok, add peanut oil, place bean sprouts in wok, and stir-fry for 1 minute over high heat. Remove from wok and drain thoroughly.
4. In a spring roll skin, place 1½ to 2 tablespoons of bean sprouts, a bit of raw shrimp, raw pork, and shredded scallions and roll closed, following steps 5, 6, and 7 of the Cantonese Spring Rolls recipe, *page 124*. Seal edges either with beaten egg or with a cornstarch-water paste mixture (see Imperial Seafood Rolls, step 5, *page 126*).

✄ Sun Tak Spring Rolls cannot be frozen, because bean sprouts wilt when frozen.

SHANGHAI CHUN GUEN
Shanghai Spring Rolls
30 rolls

30 or more Spring Roll Skins, *page 122* (or use packaged skins)
 6 ounces fresh pork, shredded
¼ pound shrimp, shelled, deveined, washed, dried, and shredded

In a small bowl, combine to make a marinade:
   ½ teaspoon salt
  1½ teaspoons sugar
    1 teaspoon sesame oil
      Pinch of white pepper
   ½ teaspoon light soy sauce
   ½ teaspoon cornstarch

 4 tablespoons peanut oil
 8 cups tightly packed celery cabbage, mostly leaves, cut lengthwise and then in ¼-inch slices
 1 tablespoon white wine
 1 teaspoon sesame oil

1.   Divide the marinade equally into 2 bowls. Add the pork to one bowl and the shrimp to the other. Marinate both for 1 hour. Drain the pork and shrimp, and reserve the marinade for use later.

2.   Heat wok for 40 seconds, then add 2 tablespoons of the peanut oil and spread it around the edges of the wok. When a wisp of white smoke appears, add the celery cabbage leaves. Stir for 1 to 2 minutes, until the leaves soften. Remove, strain, drain, and reserve the leaves.

3.   Wash the wok and dry. Heat for 40 seconds over high heat. Pour in the remaining 2 tablespoons of peanut oil. Add pork, stir-fry for 30 seconds. Make a well in the center of the pork; add the shrimp. Cook for 30 seconds, then mix thoroughly. Add white wine and mix completely.

4.   Make another well and add the marinade. Mix well and lower heat. Cook until the sauce thickens and turns dark. Turn off heat, add the sesame oil, and stir.

5.   Place the cooked pork-shrimp mixture in a shallow dish and allow it to come to room temperature. Refrigerate overnight, uncovered.

6.   Make the spring rolls, following steps 5, 6, and 7 of the Cantonese Spring Rolls recipe, *page 124.*

✁ Shanghai Spring Rolls can be frozen after cooking. To reheat, deep-fat fry lightly at 325°F. until heated through.

Meats and Vegetables: The Essence of Freshness

The essence of Cantonese cooking is that everything is fresh. Vegetables should be just picked or out of the ground, fruit right off the trees, meats only hours from being on the hoof, fish and shrimp still swimming when bought. To the Cantonese, freshness is everything; so that when spices and seasonings are added judiciously they underscore the prepared food rather than overpower it. These dim sum recipes illustrate that principle. Each of them is a happy combination of fresh ingredients and complementary seasonings.

CHAU MAI NGAU YUK YEUN	*Dry-Roasted Rice Meatballs*
PAI GWAT SIU MAI	*Spare Ribs Siu Mai*
WAN TUI SIU MAI	*Yunnan Ham Siu Mai*
WOO GOK	*Taro Root Horns*
GAI SEE GUEN	*Fresh Rice Noodle with Shredded Chicken*

CHAU MAI NGAU YUK YEUN
Dry-Roasted Rice Meatballs
20 meatballs

This is a dim sum that must be credited, at least philosophically, to Szechuan Province. It is my creation, an adaptation of a Szechuan recipe.

130

The Szechuanese use chunks of meat and coat them with dry-roasted crushed rice before steaming them. I do not fancy that taste that much. What I have done is to make small seasoned beef meatballs and coat them with roasted crushed rice and then steam them. They are one of my contributions to the dim sum repertoire.

1 cup white rice
1 pound ground beef
4 fresh water chestnuts, peeled, washed, dried, and diced
3 scallions, ends discarded, washed, dried, and finely sliced
2 teaspoons fresh minced ginger
1 egg, beaten
1½ tablespoons cornstarch mixed with 2 tablespoons cold water
1¼ teaspoons salt
2½ teaspoons sugar
1½ teaspoons sesame oil
1½ teaspoons light soy sauce
1 teaspoon blended whiskey
2 tablespoons peanut oil
Pinch of white pepper

1.   Wash and soak rice for 1 hour, drain, and dry thoroughly. In a wok, dry-roast the rice until it is golden brown. When the rice cools, layer it onto a sheet of wax paper. With a rolling pin, roll over the rice until it becomes coarse crumbs but is not powdery. Set aside on the sheet of wax paper.
2.   In the bowl of an electric mixer, combine all the remaining ingredients. Mix at low speed for 3 minutes, then at medium speed for 3 to 4 minutes, or until all ingredients are thoroughly mixed. Refrigerate for 2 to 3 hours.
3.   Grab a handful of the chilled mixture and with an open-close motion of your hand, smooth the mixture, then squeeze it so that a rounded form comes out of the thumb side of the fist and forms a ball about 1¼ inches in diameter (about the size of a Ping-Pong ball).

4. Place the ball on wax paper. Repeat until all of the mixture has been made into balls.
5. Coat a sheet of wax paper with a thin layer of the crushed rice. Pick up the meatball and roll it on the rice until it is thickly coated. Repeat until all the meatballs are coated.

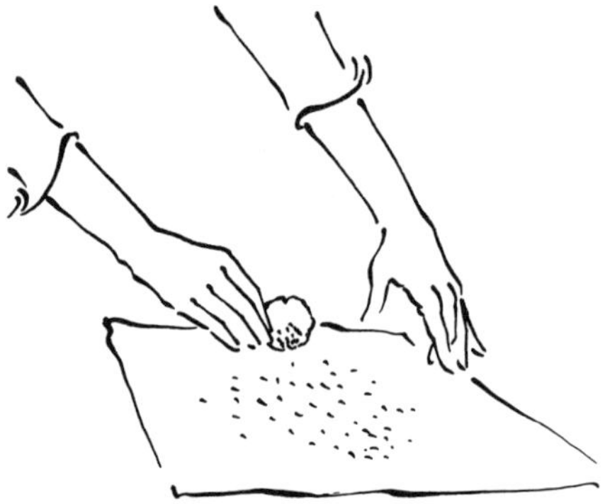

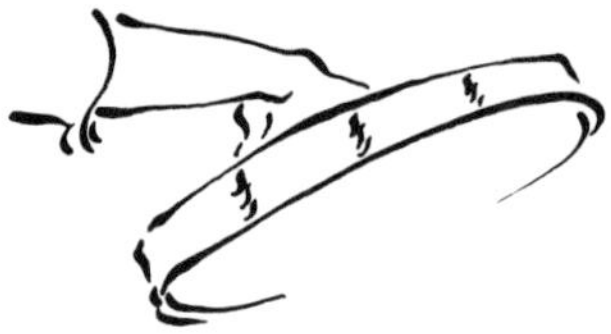

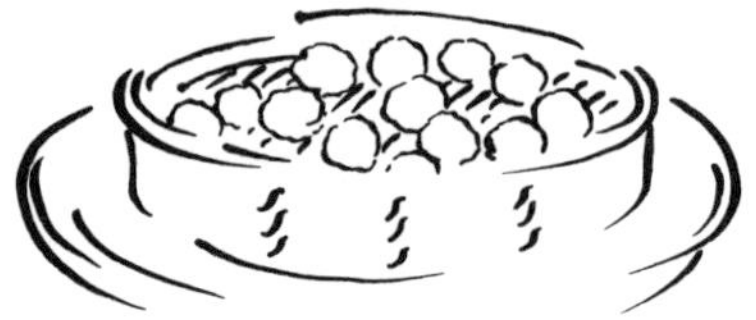

6. Place the balls on a heatproof dish, then steam them for 5 to 7 minutes. These also may be steamed right in the steamer, but the bottom must first be lined with a layer of lettuce leaves to prevent sticking. Serve immediately.

NOTE: If you do not have an electric mixer, combine the meatball ingredients in a bowl, using chopsticks to stir. Divide the mass in half, and slap each half 10 to 15 times against the side of another bowl. Repeat with the second half of the mixture. Then combine both halves and proceed as directed from step 3.

Dry-Roasted Rice Meatballs cannot be frozen.

排骨燒賣

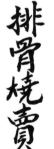

PAI GWAT SIU MAI

Spare Ribs Siu Mai

About 3 cups

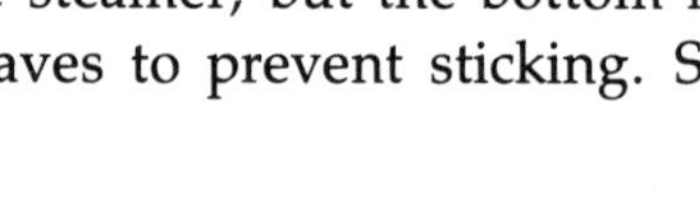

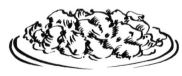

Is there anyone who does not adore Chinese-style spare ribs? Not likely, nor can a Cantonese restaurant be found that doesn't have spare ribs on the menu. But not *these* spare ribs. Dim sum–style spare ribs are neither barbecued nor broiled, but are steamed with black beans.

2¹/₂ pounds of spare ribs (net weight after cutting and trimming)

Combine in a large bowl:
>   2 teaspoons salt
>   2 tablespoons sugar
>   1 tablespoon white wine
>   2 tablespoons oyster sauce
>   1 teaspoon sesame oil
>   2 teaspoons minced garlic
>   2 tablespoons fermented black beans, washed
>   ³/₄ teaspoon baking soda
>   4 tablespoons tapioca flour
>   Pinch of white pepper
>   ¹/₄ to ¹/₂ teaspoon hot pepper flakes, or 1 tablespoon of fresh
>   hot pepper, minced
>   2 tablespoons fresh red bell peppers, sliced (optional)

1.   Trim the spare ribs and cut them into 1¹/₂-inch cubes.
2.   Add spare rib pieces to the marinade. Mix thoroughly and refrigerate overnight.
3.   Place the spare ribs and the marinade in a heatproof dish and steam for 30 minutes or until done.
4.   Place the spare ribs in a serving dish and garnish with a sprinkling of red pepper slices, if you wish. Serve immediately.

Spare ribs can be frozen. To reheat, allow to defrost to room temperature, then steam for 8 to 10 minutes or until hot.

W A N　T U I　S I U　M A I
Yunnan Ham Siu Mai
20 pieces

This dim sum is a three-province blend. It incorporates the strong cured ham of Yunnan, highly prized in China, the crisp cabbage of Tientsin, and the cooking skill of Canton. Yunnan ham is unavailable in the United States so I substitute Smithfield ham for it and this American variety substitutes quite well indeed.

    1 pound shrimp, shelled, deveined, washed, dried, and cut into 1/4-
        inch dice
    3 tablespoons pork fat, cut into 1/8-inch dice
 1 1/2 teaspoons salt
    3 teaspoons sugar
  1/2 pound lean fresh pork, coarsely ground
    3 teaspoons light soy sauce
 2 1/2 teaspoons sesame oil
    2 tablespoons oyster sauce
 1 1/2 teaspoons grated fresh ginger mixed with 2 tablespoons white
        wine
    2 tablespoons cornstarch
    1 teaspoon coriander, finely chopped
  1/2 cup Chinese black mushrooms, soaked, dried, and cut into 1/8-inch
        dice
  1/2 cup bamboo shoots, cut into 1/8-inch dice
  1/2 cup scallions, ends discarded, washed, dried, and finely sliced
      Pinch of white pepper
   20 stalks of Chinese celery cabbage
   20 slices of cooked Smithfield ham, cut into strips, 2 inches long by 1/2
        inch wide
    1 carrot, peeled, washed, dried, cut into 2-inch sections, and sliced
        into 1/8-inch-thick-, 1/2-inch-wide pieces

1.　In the bowl of an electric mixer, place the shrimp and the pork fat. Add salt and sugar; mix at medium speed for 10 minutes. Add the ground pork and mix thoroughly. Then add the soy sauce, sesame oil, oyster sauce, grated ginger mixture, and cornstarch. Mix for 5 more minutes.

2.   Add the coriander, mushrooms, bamboo shoots, scallions, and pepper. Mix together at high speed for 10 minutes, until the mixture has a thick, pasty consistency. Refrigerate this filling for 2 hours.

3.   Remove the leafy stalks, piece by piece, from a head of celery cabbage. Wash and dry thoroughly.

4.   To water-blanch the celery cabbage: Place 8 cups of water in a wok and bring to a boil. Place the cabbage leaves in the water and allow them to simmer for 3 to 4 minutes, or until softened. (It will probably be necessary to boil the leaves in 2 batches.)

5.   Remove the cabbage leaves from the boiling water and place them in a large bowl. Run the leaves under cold running water, drain, and pat dry with a paper towel.

6.   Lay a leaf stalk flat on the work surface. Place 3½ tablespoons of the filling mixture onto the leaf; on top of the meat mixture, place 2 or 3 strips of the Smithfield ham and a piece of carrot. Roll toward the leafy end of the stalk. Repeat until you have made 20 Siu Mai.

7.   Steam the Siu Mai for 15 to 20 minutes and serve immediately.

❧ Yunnan Ham Siu Mai cannot be frozen.

WOO GOK
Taro Root Horns
24 pieces

Taro root is a traditional food during the Festival of the August Moon, when it is served plain after being boiled. At New Year's it is finely sliced and fried in chips, similar to potato chips. At other times of the year it is made into dim sum—the fluffy, egg-shaped woo gok—after being steamed and then mashed. I have a particular fondness for woo gok now because I introduced my husband to it when we first met in Hong Kong. It became his favorite dim sum during our honeymoon, and after.

1½ pounds of taro root (*see note*), to yield exactly 1 pound of cooked, mashed taro
   6 ounces fresh shrimp, shelled, deveined, washed in salted water, well-dried, and diced into ⅛-inch pieces
   6 ounces fresh pork, diced into ⅛-inch pieces
   4 medium Chinese dried mushrooms, soaked in hot water for ½ hour, squeezed, stems removed, diced into ⅛-inch pieces
   ⅔ cup wheat starch
   10 ounces boiling water
   1 teaspoon salt
   1 teaspoon five-spice powder
   ⅔ cup lard
   3 tablespoons peanut oil
   2 eggs, beaten
   4 to 5 cups peanut oil for deep-fat frying

1.   Peel taro root, cut into large pieces, and steam for 1 to 1½ hours. To make certain the pieces are tender, insert a chopstick into the vegetable. If it goes in easily, the taro root is cooked. Allow to cool a bit, then mash the taro root with your fingers. It should be quite smooth.
2.   Combine shrimp, pork, and mushrooms and marinate for 30 to 60 minutes in:

  3/4 teaspoon salt
   1 teaspoon sugar
   1 teaspoon light soy sauce
  1/2 teaspoon sesame oil
1 1/2 teaspoons oyster sauce
  1/2 teaspoon blended whiskey
     Pinch of white pepper
   1 tablespoon cornstarch

3. In a mixing bowl, mix wheat starch with boiling water. As you pour
the boiling water into the mixing bowl with one hand, stir the mixture
with chopsticks with the other hand. Stir until mixture becomes a paste.
4. Add the mashed taro to the wheat-starch paste. Add salt, five-spice
powder, and lard and knead the mixture with your hands like a dough
until all ingredients are well blended. Refrigerate mixture for at least 4
hours.
5. Stir-fry marinated shrimp-pork-mushroom mixture in the 3 tablespoons
peanut oil over high heat for 1 or 2 minutes until cooked. Add beaten
eggs, lower heat, combine until the eggs are softly scrambled and mixed
with other ingredients. Remove mixture from heat, place in shallow dish,
and allow it to cool to room temperature. Refrigerate 4 hours.
6. Take 2 or 3 tablespoons of taro dough mixture, mold it into a ball,
and gently press, creating a well with your fingers.

7. Place 1 tablespoon of chilled filling in the center of the well; then,
holding woo gok in one hand, thumb in middle, turn and close with the
other hand. When hole is closed, lightly turn with 2 hands, making an
oblong-shaped form. Repeat until all the dough mixture and filling is
used.
8. Heat the 4 to 5 cups of peanut oil in wok to 350° to 375°F. Place woo
gok, 4 at a time, in wok and fry until golden brown on both sides. Drain

and serve immediately in fluted paper cups, which can be purchased at any supermarket or food store.

NOTE: The best taro root is threaded with delicate purple veins. Ask your grocer for this sort of root because it has a fine fragrance and cooks and tastes better.

❧ Woo Gok cannot be frozen, but can be prepared a day ahead. Reheat either in 350°F. oven or deep-fat fry for 1 to 2 minutes.

GAI SEE GUEN
Fresh Rice Noodle with Shredded Chicken
8 to 10 pieces

Fresh rice noodle, called "sah hor fun" by the Cantonese, comes in huge sheets and is one of the more difficult dim sum ingredients to obtain. Made from rice powder and water, it is available fresh only from bean-curd and rice-noodle factories in Asian areas of cities, or in shops that buy it specifically for sale on a specific day. It is strong and elastic, far more so than any rice noodle you might attempt to make at home. If you find that rice noodle is unavailable, you can still use this recipe. The shredded chicken filling of this dim sum will make a superb main course.

3 cups peanut oil
1/2 pound fresh pork, shredded into 1 1/2-inch lengths

½ pound chicken cutlets, boned, shredded into 1½-inch lengths
1½ cups bamboo shoots, shredded into 1½-inch lengths
⅓ cup Chinese mushrooms, soaked, washed, squeezed dry, stems
        discarded, and caps shredded
1 tablespoon white wine

In a small bowl, combine:

2½ tablespoons oyster sauce
1½ teaspoons light soy sauce
¾ teaspoon salt (optional)
1½ teaspoons sugar
   Pinch of white pepper
2 tablespoons cornstarch
¼ cup chicken broth

1 teaspoon sesame oil
2 sheets fresh rice noodle

1.   To oil-blanch filling ingredients: Heat wok over high heat, add oil, and heat to 300° to 325°F. Add pork, loosening the meat with a spatula. Add chicken, loosening the meat in the same manner. Add vegetables. Cook for 1 to 2 minutes, turn off heat, and remove contents of the wok with a Chinese strainer. Drain the contents over a large bowl. Reserve the oil left in the wok for another use.

2.   Wash the wok, place it back on stove, heat it, and dry it with a paper towel.
3.   Reheat the wok and stir-fry the meat and vegetables for 1 to 2 minutes. Add the white wine and mix well.
4.   Make a well in the center of the ingredients, pour in the sauce mixture, and mix thoroughly. When the mixture thickens, add the sesame oil.

Mix well, then place the filling in a shallow dish. Allow to cool to room temperature, then refrigerate for at least 4 hours, or overnight, before making the rice noodle rolls.

5.   Unwrap the rice noodle, roll it out with the sticky side up, and flatten it with your fingers. With a scraper, cut out skins, 6 by 6 inches. If the noodle is cracked, cut the pieces slightly larger so that the crack can be covered.

6.   Along one edge, mound a line of the filling, about 4 inches long and 1 inch in diameter. Roll tightly, trim the ends, and place on a heatproof dish or plate. Repeat until all the filling is used.

7.   Place the dish in a steamer and steam for 10 to 15 minutes, or until hot. Serve immediately.

✄ Gai See Guen may be frozen, but not after steaming. The filling may be frozen as well. Before making the dim sum, allow both to defrost and to come to room temperature, and then steam the rice noodle until it softens.

糕 餅 Unexpected Cakes

Cakes as sweet desserts are not very common among the Cantonese, who prefer fruit at the end of their meals. But they do eat sweet cakes during holidays, festivals, and at weddings. In the dim sum teahouses there will be a few sweet cakes, such as those based on water chestnut powder and sweet rice, and of course there will be those sweet, egg-yellow custard tarts that are so prized by the Cantonese. (These are a favorite of my younger son, who eats them by the plateful.) And there will be unsweetened cakes, usually made from grains and vegetables.

LOR BOK GOH	*Turnip Cake*
DZIN LOR BOK GOH	*Pan-Fried Turnip Cake*
SANG MAW MAH TAI GOH	*Water Chestnut Cake*
DZIN SANG MAW MAH TAI GOH	*Pan-Fried Water Chestnut Cake*
JAH SANG MAW MAH TAI GOH	*Batter-Fried Water Chestnut Cake*
DON TOT	*Egg Custard Tarts*
	Alternate Dough for Egg Custard Tarts

LOR BOK GOH
Turnip Cake

18–20 servings

This cake is symbolic at the time of the New Year. The cake, the "goh," represents one's job, business, or fortune, and as the cake rises during baking, one's position is said to improve.

  1 pound, 5 ounces (about 4 cups) fresh Chinese turnips
25 ounces cold water
  1 quarter-inch-thick slice of ginger, peeled and mashed
  2 tablespoons white wine
  1 whole clove garlic, peeled
     Pinch of white pepper
  1 pound of rice powder (*see note*)
  2 cups plus 2 tablespoons cold water
  2 tablespoons dried shrimp, soaked in water, then diced into 1/4-inch
        pieces
1/3 cup Chinese sausage (lop cheung), diced into 1/4-inch pieces
1/3 cup Chinese bacon, diced into 1/4-inch pieces
1/4 teaspoon white pepper
  1 tablespoon salt
1/2 cup liquefied pork fat

   Garnishes:
        1 to 2 tablespoons sesame seeds, dry-roasted
        4 to 6 scallions, finely sliced
        1 tablespoon coriander, finely minced (optional)

1.   Wash and peel the turnips. Grate them coarsely.
2.   In a large pot, place the turnips, the 25 ounces of cold water, and the ginger, white wine, garlic, and the pinch of white pepper. Cover and bring to a boil over high heat. Lower heat and simmer, with lid partially open, for 20 minutes. Remove the turnip mixture from the stove, allow it to cool, then discard the ginger and the garlic.
3.   In a large mixing bowl, mix rice powder with 2 cups of the water. (Use the extra 2 tablespoons of water *only* if the rice powder does not absorb the 2 cups.) Add the dried shrimp, sausage, bacon, 1/4 teaspoon

of white pepper, salt, and the pork fat. Mix well, then add cooked turnips and mix well again.

4.   In a greased 9-inch-square cake pan, place the turnip mixture and steam for 1 to 1½ hours. To discern whether the cake is cooked, insert a chopstick into the center. If the chopstick is clean when pulled out, the cake is done. If a residue remains, continue to steam until the cake tests done.

5.   Remove the cake from the steamer and allow it to cool slightly. Just before serving, sprinkle on the dry-roasted sesame seeds, then the minced scallions, and finally the optional coriander. Serve immediately in slices, as you would a cake.

NOTE: Be certain to use *rice powder* and *not* glutinous *rice*, which comes in a similar wrapping.

❧ Turnip Cake cannot be frozen, but can be refrigerated either whole or in slices. To reheat, allow the cake to return to room temperature, then steam for 20 to 30 minutes or until heated through. Also, the cake can be pan-fried. (See Pan-Fried Turnip Cake, *page 144.*)

DZIN LOR BOK GOH
Pan-Fried Turnip Cake
18–20 servings

Some people prefer their turnip cake sliced thin and then pan-fried—and it is delicious this way. If you wish to pan-fry it, prepare the cake a day before you plan to serve it and refrigerate it overnight. Eliminate the sesame seed and the scallion garnishes, since both will "pop" fiercely during the frying process. You may, however, garnish the pan-fried turnip cake with coriander.

1. Prepare one Turnip Cake, *page 142*.
2. Cut the cake into slices, 1/4 inch thick by 2 1/2 inches long, and 2 inches wide. Fry in peanut oil until light brown. Drain, and serve immediately.

SANG MAW MAH TAI GOH
Water Chestnut Cake
18–20 servings

This totally vegetarian preparation is highly esteemed in China. Not only is it tasty, but it is versatile and can be enjoyed in 3 distinctive ways. Chinese grandmothers like the combination of water chestnuts and sugar very much and feed it to their grandchildren incessantly, not only as a system purifier when they have the measles, but at all other times as well.

1 1/4-pound can of water chestnuts (*see note*)
1 1/2 to 1 3/4 cups sugar
3 3/4 cups boiling water
1/2 pound water chestnut powder
1 cup cold water

1. Drain water chestnuts, dice fine, and set aside.
2. Dissolve sugar in boiling water and set aside.
3. In a large mixing bowl, mix water chestnut powder with cold water. Add the sugar water and the diced water chestnuts and mix well.

4.   Pour the contents into a wok, and heat over a medium flame. Using a metal spatula, stir continuously in one direction for 5 to 7 minutes, until the mixture is very thick and pasty.

5.   Grease a 9-inch square cake pan generously with peanut oil. Pour the chestnut mixture into the pan and place it in a steamer. Steam the cake for 30 to 45 minutes, until it is firmly gelled and takes on a translucent quality. Slice as you would a cake, and serve.

NOTE: A 1¼-pound can supplies the same amount of ready-to-use water chestnuts as 2 pounds of fresh ones. For this cake, canned water chestnuts are as good as the fresh and save about an hour's worth of peeling time.

Water Chestnut Cake can be enjoyed in 2 other ways, pan-fried or batter-fried. In each case, the cake must be made a day earlier and refrigerated. See Pan-Fried Water Chestnut Cake, *page 145*; or Batter-Fried Water Chestnut Cake, *page 146.*

➳ Water Chestnut Cake can be frozen, either whole or in slices. To reheat, allow the cake to return to room temperature, then steam for 15 to 20 minutes or until heated through. Also, after defrosting, the cake can be pan-fried or batter-fried.

D Z I N   S A N G   M A W   M A H   T A I   G O H
Pan-Fried Water Chestnut Cake
18–20 servings

1.   Prepare Water Chestnut Cake, *page 144*, 1 day ahead of time. Refrigerate the unsliced cake.

2.   Cut the chilled cake into ¼-inch by 2½-inch by 2-inch slices. Pour 2 to 3 tablespoons of peanut oil into a 9-inch cast-iron skillet. Heat over high heat until a wisp of white smoke appears. Pan-fry the cake slices, 3 or 4 at a time, until golden brown. Drain and serve immediately.

JAH SANG MAW MAH TAI GOH
Batter-Fried Water Chestnut Cake
18–20 servings

    1 Water Chestnut Cake, *page 144*, prepared a day ahead, unsliced
        and refrigerated
 1/2 cup flour (Pillsbury's All-Purpose preferred)
 1/2 cup cornstarch
2 1/2 teaspoons baking powder
    5 ounces cold water
    1 tablespoon peanut oil

1.   In a large mixing bowl, combine the dry ingredients and mix well.
Add the cold water while stirring continuously with chopsticks or a
wooden spoon, until batter is well blended. Then add peanut oil and
mix until the oil is blended in well. If the batter seems too thick, add a
bit more water.
2.   Heat 4 to 5 cups of peanut oil in a wok to 350° to 375°F.
3.   Slice the Water Chestnut Cake into pieces 2 1/2 inches by 1 inch by 1
inch. Dip in batter with chopsticks or tongs. Place slices in oil, 3 or 4 at
a time, and cook, turning, for about 2 or 3 minutes, or until the pieces
are golden. Drain and serve immediately.

DON TOT
Egg Custard Tarts
20 tarts

Egg Custard Tarts are a favorite dim sum with the Chinese people. Traditionally, they are served warm. However, some people (like my husband)
like them cold. To me, they are delicious either way.

Mixture 1
 1 cup Gold Medal flour
 1/4 cup Pillsbury's High-Gluten Flour
 1 large egg

4 tablespoons lard
2 ounces water

Place both the flours on the work surface, make a well in the center, and add the egg. Work the egg and the flour together with your fingers until the egg is absorbed. Add the lard and work in thoroughly with your fingers. Gradually dribble in the water (add an additional 1 or 2 tablespoons if mixture seems too dry) and combine. Using a dough scraper to pick up the dough, knead for 20 minutes, until the dough is well combined. Refrigerate for 30 minutes.

Mixture 2
4 tablespoons butter
4 tablespoons margarine
4 tablespoons lard
1/2 cup plus 1/3 cup Gold Medal flour

Place butter, margarine, and lard in a bowl and cream together until smooth. Add the flour and mix until the consistency of icing is achieved. Refrigerate for 30 minutes.

Filling ingredients
3 cups boiling water
1 cup sugar
6 eggs, beaten
1/4 teaspoon pure vanilla extract
1/2 cup evaporated milk

To make the filling
Bring water to a boil in a 2-quart saucepan. Add the sugar and stir until dissolved. Turn off the heat and allow the mixture to cool to room temperature. In a bowl, beat the eggs and add the vanilla and the evaporated milk. Beat until thoroughly mixed. Add the cooled sugar water to the egg mixture and beat again. Remove the bubbles and set the mixture aside.

To make the tarts
1.   Sprinkle flour on the work surface and on a rolling pin. Roll out

Dough 1 to a piece 17 by 16 inches. Remove Dough 2 from the refrigerator, flatten it, and place it in the middle of the rolled out Dough 1.

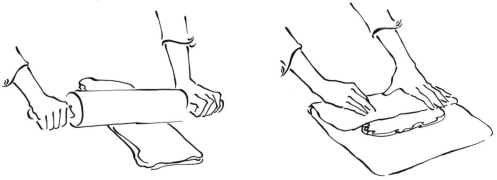

2.   Pick up the ends of the rolled out Dough 1, fold them in, and press them down gently on top of Dough 2 to create a sealed envelope. Dust the rolling pin and the work surface again with flour and roll out the combined doughs to a piece 18 inches square.

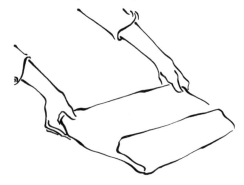

3.   Fold the dough in thirds and roll it out a second time to a piece about 18 inches square. Then fold it in quarters, making certain to dust the surface, dough, and rolling pin with flour, and roll it out a third time to a piece about 18 inches square and about 1/4 inch thick.

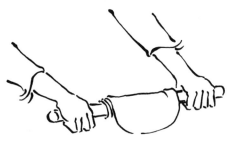

4. Using a 4-inch cookie cutter, cut out circles 4 inches in diameter (smaller if your custard tins are smaller) and stack the circles in a pile. Wrap them in plastic wrap and refrigerate them for 1 hour. Gather the dough remnants, knead, roll out, and repeat until all the dough is used.

5. Place the circles of dough into 3½-inch fluted tart tins. Press the dough down gently with thumbs, making certain that it is pressed firmly into the fluting and on the bottoms. Pour the filling into the tart tins; fill to about ¼ inch from the tops.

6. Preheat oven to 375°F. Place the tins on cookie sheets, then bake for 30 minutes or until crusts are brown and the filling thickens. Serve immediately.

✄ Egg Custard Tarts can be frozen after baking, and they will keep for 4 to 6 weeks in the freezer. To reheat, place in tart tins, defrost, and allow the tarts to come to room temperature. Heat in a 325°F. oven until warm.

DON TOT
Alternate Dough for Egg Custard Tarts

Mixture 1

1¼ cups Gold Medal flour
2 ounces butter
1 large egg
2½ ounces cold water

Bring the butter to room temperature, and cream it thoroughly. Place the flour on the work surface, make a well in the center, and add creamed butter and the egg. Using your fingertips and stirring in 1 direction, mix the ingredients together, letting butter and egg absorb the flour. Slowly dribble water into dough and work with fingers to mix well. Knead for 2 minutes. Sprinkle surface with flour to avoid sticking. Wrap dough in plastic wrap and refrigerate for 30 minutes.

Mixture 2

6 ounces butter at room temperature
¼ pound Gold Medal flour

Cream butter in bowl and add flour. Mix until it becomes like icing, then refrigerate for 30 minutes. Using these 2 doughs, follow the instructions for making Egg Custard Tarts, *page 146*.

NOTE: Because only butter is used, instead of lard and margarine, these dough circles need to be refrigerated for only 30 minutes, since butter will harden more quickly than lard or margarine.

Sculptured Dim Sum

Sculptured dim sum is a special art of the city of Suzhou, or Sochow, as it is known to the Cantonese. Culinary artistry is commonplace in this beautiful whitewashed city of canals, and a special meal or banquet is as lovely to look at as it is to eat. Every course invariably includes birds, frogs, fish, and flowers—all sculpted in dough and steamed to translucence. Some of these are meant to be eaten, others simply serve as decorations to please the eye or to highlight the presentation of other foods. In any case, all are feasts.

Not only are sculptured dim sum beautiful to look at, they happen to be surprisingly simple to make—quite reminiscent of playing with modeling clay, as when you were a child. The dough is the same for all recipes, and it is a simple one, as you will see in the Basic Dough recipe on *page 153*.

Dim sum sculptures can be filled with any one of several fillings. I have provided a Basic Meat Filling on *page 154*. You can also use Bean Paste Filling (I recommend using canned bean paste, although you can make your own from the recipe on *page 76*) or Lotus Seed Paste Filling. Or, you can simply stuff each sculpture with a piece of the skin dough.

Particularly when you begin making dim sum sculptures, I suggest that you use the skin dough as filling. Although you will find that sculpting, in the end, is rather easy, you will surely make mistakes in the beginning. I did. It could prove both wasteful and expensive to have stuffed them with the meat or either of the pastes. Also, to my mind, sculpted dim sum are not quite as delicious as other dim sum, if only because of the thickness of the sculpting dough. Thus, the dough should serve as an adequate filling for what will be, essentially, a decoration.

You will need a few extra pieces of equipment for making dim sum sculptures:

A 4-inch round cookie cutter: I recommend that you use a cookie cutter to cut out the basic circle that each sculpture requires. Your sculptures will be prettier and easier to make if you begin with a perfect circle.

Food coloring: In many of these recipes, I recommend that you paint the edges and ridges of some of the sculptures to make them more beautiful as well as more realistic. For these recipes, you will need red, yellow, and green food coloring.

A small brush: In order to highlight the edges of the sculptures, you will need a small brush. You can buy such a brush at an art store or dime store. I tried several types and ended up using a lipstick brush I had around the house. It was the perfect size.

From one basic dough recipe, you can make 2 or 3 of each of the recipes that follow. It looks difficult, I know, but these are a great pleasure to make. And, if you wish to eat them in the end, you can be assured of dining on a true Chinese delicacy.

✄ A Note About Freezing

All of the sculptures can be frozen, but only if you wish to use them later for decoration. They are tasty when freshly cooked (especially the Four-Seasons Dim Sum), but lose most of their flavor after freezing. To reheat, allow them to return to room temperature, then steam them for 8 to 10 minutes, or until they are warmed through. They should be reheated, even if they are going to be used only for decoration, as they will appear more beautiful this way.

Basic Dough for Dim Sum Sculptures
Basic Meat Filling
Red Bean Paste Filling
Lotus Seed Paste Filling
Four-Seasons Dim Sum

Goldfish Sculpture
Orchid Sculpture
Dove Sculpture
Butterfly Sculpture
Frog Sculpture

BASIC DOUGH FOR DIM SUM SCULPTURES

20 to 30 sculptures

   2 cups Pillsbury's All-Purpose Flour
 3/4 teaspoon baking soda
 1/2 to 1 teaspoon salt
   1 cup boiling water
      Cornstarch for dusting

1.   In a large mixing bowl, place the flour, baking soda, and salt. While stirring constantly with chopsticks, slowly add the boiling water. Continue stirring constantly until all of the flour has absorbed all the liquid.

2.   When the dough is cool enough to handle, knead it in the bowl or on a work surface for 5 to 7 minutes, or until it forms a smooth ball. Cover it with plastic wrap and allow it to rest for 1 hour.
3.   After the dough has rested, dust the work surface and your hands generously with cornstarch.
4.   Divide the dough in half. Set one half aside, covered with a piece of plastic wrap. Roll the second half into a log about 10 inches in length. Using a scraper, divide the log into 10 equal pieces, each about 1 inch long. Cover the pieces with a sheet of plastic wrap until you are ready to work with them.

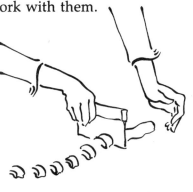
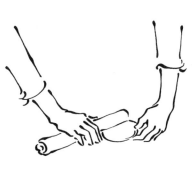

BASIC MEAT FILLING
Fills 20 to 30 sculptures

  1 pound fresh ground pork
  1/4 pound shrimp, shelled, deveined, washed in salted water, drained, dried, and finely diced
  3 scallions, ends discarded, washed, dried thoroughly, and finely chopped
  2 cloves garlic, minced
  1/2 cup water chestnuts, peeled, washed, dried, and cut into 1/8-inch dice
  1 tablespoon grated ginger mixed into 1 tablespoon white wine
  1 1/2 teaspoons salt
  1 1/2 teaspoons sugar
  1 1/2 teaspoons light soy sauce
  1 1/2 teaspoons sesame oil
  1 1/2 teaspoons oyster sauce
    Pinch of white pepper
  3 to 4 tablespoons cornstarch
  1 egg

1. In a large mixing bowl, combine all of these ingredients. Using 2 chopsticks, stir clockwise continuously until all the ingredients are blended smoothly.
2. Refrigerate for 3 or 4 hours before using (chilled filling is easier to work with).

RED BEAN PASTE FILLING
Fills 20 to 30 sculptures

For a bean paste filling, you can use commercial canned bean paste, or make the bean paste from scratch, using the recipe on *page 76*.

LOTUS SEED PASTE FILLING
Fills 20 to 30 sculptures

$^1/_2$ pound dried lotus seeds
$^3/_4$ cup lard
$^3/_4$ cup sugar

1.   In a large mixing bowl, place the dried lotus seeds. Fill the bowl with enough warm water to cover the seeds. Allow them to soak for 6 to 8 hours, or overnight.
2.   Drain the water from the soaked lotus seeds. Place the lotus seeds in a large pot, together with 5 cups of cold water. Cover the pot, and bring the water to a boil. Reduce the heat, partially uncover the pot, and allow it to simmer for 4 to 5 hours, or until all of the water is absorbed by the lotus seeds.
3.   Using a potato masher, mash the seeds in the pot, or transfer the seeds to the bowl of a food processor and mash. If you use a food processor, you must divide the seeds into 4 batches, and mash $^1/_4$ at a time.
4.   In another pot, melt the lard, then add the sugar. Stir over low heat for 3 minutes, until the mixture is smooth. Add the mashed lotus seeds, stirring constantly, and cook for 45 minutes to 1 hour over low to medium heat, until the paste has the consistency of wet sand. If the heat is too high, the paste will burn, so check it occasionally, and lower the heat if necessary.
5.   Remove the lotus paste from the stove and allow it to cool. Then transfer the paste to a container and refrigerate until ready to use.

❧ This extremely rich filling will keep for 4 to 6 weeks in your refrigerator.

SEI GUAI DIM SUM
Four-Seasons Dim Sum

30 sculptures

Of all the dim sum sculptures, this one is particularly delicious to eat. It is also especially attractive to look at and therefore is often used as a decoration. It symbolizes, through its clover shape and its ingredients, the 4 seasons of the year—the green vegetable leaves for spring, the red cured ham for summer, the yellow eggs for fall, and the black mushrooms for winter. Because of its varied colors, this is especially prized not only as a special dim sum, but as the first course for important banquets.

    1 Basic Dough recipe, *page 153*
    1 Basic Meat Filling recipe, *page 154*
3/4 cup (2 to 3 slices) Virginia or baked ham
3/4 cup (6 leaves) bok choy, spinach, or lettuce, water-blanched
    2 to 3 hard-boiled egg yolks
3/4 cup (about 12) Chinese black dried mushrooms, soaked, washed,
        and squeezed dry of excess water
    1 teaspoon dark soy sauce
    1 teaspoon sugar
1/2 teaspoon sesame oil
    Cornstarch for dusting

1.   Dice the ham finely, chop the green vegetable finely, and press the egg yolks through a sieve. Place each in a separate dish and set aside.
2.   In a heatproof dish, combine the dark soy sauce, the sugar, and the sesame oil. Add the mushrooms and steam for 10 minutes. Allow the mushrooms to return to room temperature, then dice them finely. Place them in a small dish and set aside.
3.   Dust the work surface with cornstarch. Roll out the dough and divide it into 4 equal pieces. Work with one, covering the rest with plastic wrap until you are ready to use them. Roll each piece into a section 15 inches long. Cut into 15 equal pieces. Cover those not being used with plastic wrap. Roll each small piece into a ball, press down with palm, dust rolling pin with cornstarch, and roll out a circle 3 inches in diameter.

To form the dumpling
1.   Place 1 to 2 teaspoons of filling in the center of the circle. Using both

hands, fold the dough in half to form a half-moon or crescent shape. With your index fingers, press the outer corners in to form 4 holes. Pinch the center of the **X** where the holes meet to hold the shape. Using your fingers, mold the dumplings to form 4 even holes. Keep your fingers coated with cornstarch at all times to avoid their sticking to the dough.

2.   Using a small spoon, such as an espresso or demitasse spoon, fill each of the 4 holes with a different filling: the red ham, the green vegetable, the yellow egg yolk, and the black mushrooms. Repeat until all the dumplings are filled.

3.   When all the dumplings have been filled, steam them for 10 to 12 minutes. Serve hot, immediately, or allow them to return to room temperature if they are to be decorations.

G O L D F I S H   S C U L P T U R E
20 sculptures

1 Basic Dough recipe, *page 153*
  Cornstarch for dusting
1 Basic Meat Filling recipe, *page 154*
40 cherries (2 for the eyes of each goldfish)
  Red or orange food coloring

Roll out a piece of dough into a circle 4 inches in diameter. Use a 4-inch cookie cutter to make a perfect circle. Dust the circle lightly with cornstarch.

To form the sculpture
1.   Fold over ⅓ of the circle. Place the circle in the palm of your hand with the folded side down. Place 1 teaspoon of the filling slightly off-

center, toward the fold. Fold up the 2 ends and form a seam on the folded edge by pinching the dough together with your thumb and forefinger. Make sure the seam is firm and closed.

2.   Turn the fish. To form the back fin, with the thumb and the index finger, pinch a pleat or ridge down the top edge of the goldfish. Make sure the seam is sealed tightly. To form side pleats, pinch 2 pleats, pushing toward the filling. To form the eye holes, pinch the dough and mold. Gently unfold and pull out the folded portion to form the tail.

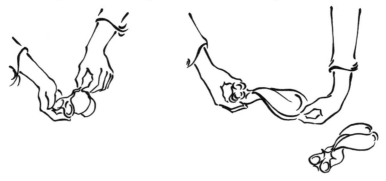

3.   Repeat until all the dough is used. Steam the goldfish for 10 to 12 minutes.

4. *To finish:* Rinse the cherries carefully to remove any excess coloring and place them in the eye holes. Using red or orange food coloring and a small brush, draw dots around the edge of the tail.

ORCHID SCULPTURE
20 sculptures

1 Basic Dough recipe, *page 153*
  Cornstarch for dusting
1 Basic Meat Filling recipe, *page 154*
  Red food coloring
  Yellow food coloring

Roll out a piece of dough into a circle, 4 inches in diameter. Cut the circle with a 4-inch cookie cutter to create a perfect circle. Dust the circle with cornstarch.

To form the sculpture

1. Fold the dough circle in thirds to form a triangle. With the folded side down, place the dough in the palm of your hand. Place a teaspoon of filling in the center of the triangle.

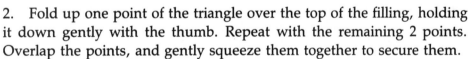

2. Fold up one point of the triangle over the top of the filling, holding it down gently with the thumb. Repeat with the remaining 2 points. Overlap the points, and gently squeeze them together to secure them.

3. Pinch a seam or ridge along each of the 3 openings. Make sure the seams are sealed firmly and the openings are tightly closed.

4. Turn the flower over and gently unfold the corners to form the petals. Mold the flower gently until it forms its final shape.

5. Steam the flowers for 12 to 15 minutes. Allow them to return to room temperature to use as decorations.

6. *To finish:* Using yellow food coloring and a small paintbrush, paint a thin yellow line down the center of each petal. Then, using red food coloring and another brush, paint a red line around the edge of each petal.

雕
刻
乳
鴿

D O V E S C U L P T U R E

20 sculptures

1 Basic Dough recipe, *page 153*
1 Basic Meat Filling recipe, *page 154*
6 Chinese black mushrooms, soaked, washed, and squeezed of excess
    water
Black sesame seeds, 2 for each bird's eyes
Cornstarch for dusting
Red food coloring

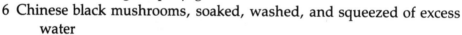

Roll out a piece of dough into a circle 4 inches in diameter. Use a 4-inch cookie cutter to create a perfect circle. Place 1 teaspoon of filling in the center of the circle.

To form the sculpture

1. *The bird's body:* Using both hands, fold the dough to form a half-moon or crescent shape. With your index fingers, press the outer corners in to

form an **X**. Pinch the middle of the **X** with the thumb and index finger to secure the top. Make sure that your fingers are coated generously with cornstarch. Form a ridge on the back of the bird by pinching the 2 hind holes together.

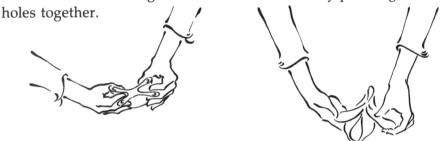

2.   *The bird's wings:* Pinch closed the openings on each of the 2 hind holes. Using your fingers, mold each flap into a wing shape by flattening the dough and pressing it forward.

3.   *The bird's head:* Pinch the front opening closed and quickly shape a head and beak. (This sounds difficult, but it is very easy.)

4.   *The bird's tail:* Remove the stems from the Chinese black mushrooms and slice them into a thin julienne. Using your fingers, enlarge the opening at the bird's tail end. Insert 5 or 6 mushroom slivers, then squeeze the dough around the slivers to hold them firmly.

5.   Using a pair of scissors, snip the edge of each wing to give it a feathered texture. Wet a chopstick and touch each side of the bird's head,

wet the chopstick again and pick up 1 sesame seed with the edge and gently press the seed to the head to form the eyes.

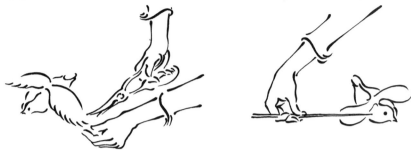

6.   When all the dumplings have been formed, steam them for 10 to 12 minutes.

7.   *To finish:* Using red food coloring and a small brush, add a bit of color to outline the bird's beak and to decorate its head.

BUTTERFLY SCULPTURE
20 sculptures

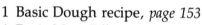

   1 Basic Dough recipe, *page 153*
   1 Basic Meat Filling recipe, *page 154*
     Cornstarch for dusting
   2 carrots, cut into fine julienne, 2 inches long by 1/8 inch thick
   1/4 pound shrimp, shelled, deveined, washed, dried, and minced to
        form a paste
   2 egg yolks, hard-boiled and pushed through a sieve
  40 peas, 2 for the eyes of each butterfly

Roll out a small piece of the dough into a circle 4 inches in diameter. Use a 4-inch cookie cutter to create a perfect circle.

To form the sculpture

1.   Place 1 teaspoon of filling in the center of the circle. Keep your fingers coated with cornstarch at all times to avoid their sticking to the dough. Using both hands, fold the dough to form a half-moon or crescent shape.

With your index fingers, press the outer corners in to form 4 holes. To hold the shape, pinch the center of the **X** where the holes meet. Using your fingers, mold the holes into the shape of butterfly wings. Pinch the edges where the wings are formed to be sure the shape will hold firmly.

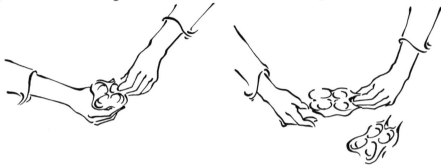

2.   *To finish:* Into the 2 "front" areas of the butterfly, place a piece of carrot. Using a small spoon, such as a demitasse or espresso spoon, fill the holes with shrimp paste, securing the carrot pieces. Fill the 2 back openings with the sieved egg yolk. Place 2 green peas in the shrimp paste to form the butterfly's eyes.

3.   When all the dumplings have been formed, steam them for 10 to 12 minutes.

FROG SCULPTURE
20 sculptures

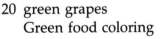

    1 Basic Dough recipe, *page 153*
    1 Basic Meat Filling recipe, *page 154*
      Cornstarch for dusting
  20 green grapes
      Green food coloring

Roll out a small piece of dough into a circle 4 inches in diameter. Use a 4-inch cookie cutter to create a perfect circle.

To form the sculpture

1.   Place 1 teaspoon of filling onto the dough circle, slightly off-center. Holding the circle in both hands, fold it into a half-moon or crescent

shape. Using your index fingers, press the outer corners in to form 4 holes. Pinch the center of the **X** where the holes meet to hold the shape.

2.   *The eyes:* Dust your fingers with cornstarch, then mold the 2 smaller holes to create a larger round space where the grapes can be inserted after the frog has been steamed.

3.   *The hind legs:* Pinch the larger holes closed, then continue pinching down each seam until a flap is formed. Fold the flap down and mold it to create the legs. With kitchen scissors, clip the edges to form toes.

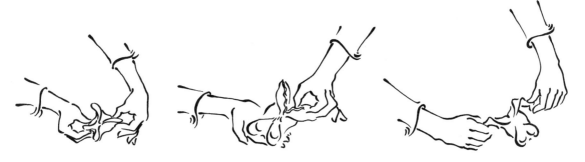

4.   Steam the frogs for 10 to 12 minutes. Allow them to return to room temperature.

5.   *To finish:* Slice the grapes in half and insert them in the eye holes to form the eyes. With green food coloring and a small brush, paint a thin line down the back ridge of each of the frogs' legs.

A Collection of Sauces

In Canton the use of sauces and oils with dim sum, especially those that "heat the mouth," is regarded as almost sinful, because the Cantonese believe that food perfectly prepared requires no enhancement.

I recall when I was very little and went reaching for some hot oil to sprinkle on some spring rolls, my grandmother glared at me and stopped my hand in midair with a call of "Barbarian!"

These days, however, the Cantonese, like most everybody else, use some sauces and oils for their dim sum, including a few that are spicy and hot. So I have included those I like and I have recommended specific sauces for specific dishes. However, there are sufficient dishes, as well as sufficient sauces, for you to experiment with. I know that many of my students prefer their dim sum with sauces that I wouldn't dream of using, but I suppose this is because I suspect my grandmother would again become angry with me. In any case, these sauces are but one more example of the adventure to be found in dim sum.

CHUNG YAU	*Scallion Oil*
TIHM CHUNG YAU	*Sweet Scallion Sauce*
LOT YAU	*Hot Oil*
SEE CHO YAU	*Vinegar Soy Sauce*
GEUNG CHUNG YAU	*Ginger Soy Sauce*
GAI LOT	*Hot Mustard*

165

CHUNG YAU
Scallion Oil

3 cups

Scallion oil is less an accompaniment than it is an ingredient. It is used in several recipes and is a base for other sauces.

1 cup of the stringy whiskers end of the scallions, washed and dried
    thoroughly
1 cup of green portion of scallions, cut into 3 sections, washed and
    dried thoroughly
3 cups peanut oil

1.   Heat wok over medium heat. Add peanut oil, then add all scallions. When the scallions turn brown, the oil is done.
2.   With a strainer, remove scallions and discard. Strain the oil through a fine strainer into a mixing bowl and allow it to cool to room temperature.
3.   Pour the scallion oil into a glass jar and refrigerate until needed.

TIHM CHUNG YAU
Sweet Scallion Sauce

About 1 cup

¼ cup Scallion Oil, *see above*
½ cup dark soy sauce
3½ tablespoons sugar
  3 tablespoons cold water

1.   Heat wok over medium heat. Pour in Scallion Oil, soy sauce, sugar, and water. Stir clockwise until all ingredients are mixed thoroughly and begin to boil.
2.   Turn the heat off. Pour the sauce into a bowl and allow it to cool to room temperature. Pour into a glass jar and refrigerate until needed.

Recommended for:
Fresh Rice Noodle with Shredded Chicken, *page 138*
My students seem to enjoy this sauce with a great number of the

various dim sum. Although it is not a sauce I would use frequently, try it with the dim sum of your choice to see if it suits your particular taste.

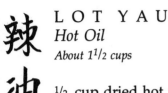

L O T   Y A U
Hot Oil
About 1½ cups

½ cup dried hot red pepper flakes
¾ cup sesame oil
¾ cup peanut oil

1.   Place all the ingredients in a large jar and mix well.
2.   Close the jar tightly and place in a cool, dry place for 4 weeks. The oil will then be ready for use.

Recommended for:
Vegetarian Dumplings, *page 57*
Water Dumplings, *page 60*
Stuffed Lotus Leaves, *page 96*
Lettuce Congee, *page 109*
Stuffed Crab Claws, *page 113*
Round Shrimp, *page 114*
Pepper Siu Mai, *page 118*

NOTE: If you don't feel like waiting several weeks, commercial hot oil is sold in Chinese grocery stores under many names, including Hunan hot oil.

SEE CHO YAU
Vinegar Soy Sauce
About 1/4 cup

Although this can be made ahead, I prefer to make it as needed so that it will be at full strength.

> 1 tablespoon dark soy sauce
> 1 tablespoon light soy sauce
> 1 tablespoon white vinegar
> 1/2 teaspoon hot oil
> 1 tablespoon finely sliced scallions, white and green portions, washed and thoroughly dried

1.   Combine all ingredients in a small bowl. Mix well.
2.   Allow the mixture to marinate for 1/2 hour, and place in a small soy sauce dish. Serve immediately.

Recommended for:
Shanghai Dumplings or Little Dumplings, *page 86*
Beef Congee, *page 108*
Stuffed Crab Claws, *page 113*
Round Shrimp, *page 114*
Dry-Roasted Rice Meatballs, *page 130*

GEUNG CHUNG YAU
Ginger Soy Sauce
About 1/4 cup

To ensure the best flavor, I prefer to make this as needed, instead of ahead of time.

> 1 teaspoon sugar
> 1/2 tablespoon dark soy sauce
> 1/2 tablespoon light soy sauce
> 1 teaspoon scallion oil
> 1 teaspoon cold water

¹/₂ tablespoon sesame oil
¹/₂ tablespoon shredded fresh ginger root
¹/₂ tablespoon of white portion of scallion, sliced thinly into ¹/₂-inch
     lengths
A *generous* pinch of white pepper

1. Combine all ingredients in a small bowl. Mix well.
2. Allow to stand for ¹/₂ hour, then serve.

Recommended for:
Scallion Pancakes, *page 82*
Fish Congee, *page 107*
Stuffed Bean Curd, *page 115*
Stuffed Mushrooms, *page 116*

GAI LOT
Hot Mustard

This is made simply by mixing equal amounts of mustard powder and
cold tap water. There are many hot mustards on the market but I prefer
the English-made Colman's Mustard, Double Superfine Compound. It
must be the dried mustard, not the Colman's prepared mustard that
comes in jars.

For a normal dim sum recipe, you will use about 2 to 3 teaspoons of
mustard to a similar amount of water.

In dim sum teahouses, small dishes, called soy dishes, are often filled
half with mixed mustard, half with a sauce of red chili paste. These tiny
dishes, which are served on request only, are quite decorative.

Mustard, however, can be served alone. Chili paste can also be served
alone. If it is unavailable, Tabasco sauce is an admirable substitute.

Recommended for:
Glutinous Rice Dough Dumplings, *page 100*
Stuffed Crab Claws, *page 113*
Shrimp Toast, *page 118*
Yunnan Ham Siu Mai, *page 134*
Taro Root Horns, *page 136*
Turnip Cake, *page 142*

HO HO SIK
A Few Last Words

It is my hope not only that you have enjoyed my book, but that you will *continue* to use and enjoy it. Although it is a cookery book, I have also touched on some customs of the Chinese in general, and of the Cantonese in particular, to tell you a bit about how they live, what they believe, their food, their teahouses, and their teas. Most important, however, I hope I have imparted to you some sense of the ever-changing nature, the vigor, and the adaptability of Chinese cooking and the deep respect for good food that is so much a part of Chinese life.

The Cantonese would say *Ho Ho Sik*, or good eating!

—Eileen Yin-Fei Lo

171

Index

Eileen Yin-Fei Lo was born in Canton, China. She came to the United States in 1959 when she married Fred Ferretti, now a feature writer for the *New York Times*. Ms. Lo has taught Cantonese cooking in her own home for years, and for the past five years she has been an instructor at the China Institute in New York City. She is well known as a food journalist, having published articles on Chinese cuisine in the *New York Times*, *Travel & Leisure*, *Diversion*, and *Intrepids*. She lives in Montclair, New Jersey, with her husband and their children, Christopher, Elena, and Stephen.